A FAITH THAT WORKS

LINWOOD JACKSON, JR.

PUBLISHED BY FIDELI PUBLISHING, INC.

ISBN: 978-1-955622-21-9 (hardcover)
978-1-955622-20-2 (paperback)

Cover image by: Fatima Azhar

For more information,
email the author at LinwoodJackson@hotmail.com,
or visit linwoodjacksonjr.com

Published by
Fideli Publishing, Inc.

www.FideliPublishing.com

PRINTED IN THE UNITED STATES OF AMERICA

Contents

Introduction

1. A right form of benevolence, or of empathy, doesn't seem to be a natural operation to the structure of the human being. It appears as though the human being is actually born unconscious to any trait confessing self-sacrificing love, seeing as how, as opposed to another's, it is easier to see the world through self's lens. And the obvious fact that we cannot ever know the thoughts and feelings of another is evident, the exercise of comprehending another's thoughts and feelings, and for understanding their words and actions to better care for them, also not being natural; this too is even more than evident.

2. The highest form of intelligence is a benevolent self-sacrificing love. This is the highest form of intelligence because this practice shows the result of what training the nature of the human being has passed through. When self is no longer the idol, and when self's assessment has led to a more thoughtful and charitable assessment of another's self, to assist that mind in kindly managing its own self, then the highest form of intelligence is demonstrated, even as it says, "Whom if thou bring forward on their journey after a godly sort, thou shalt do well."[1]

3. It is not only abnormal to embrace the anger, pain, sorrow, confusion, frustration, or joy of another, but to also consciously care to do so. This human being is naturally unconscious to such a manner of service and, can you blame it? When born, the *being* of the human grows and develops within a body, making its first experiences with life both physical and sensual. The human being, constrained to such an

---

1   3 John 1:6

v

uneducated mind within the body, and being unaware of the difference between mental and physical stimulus, will naturally interpret all things through the body's physical *brain*, leaving that other more elevated portion of its nature to suffer without use.

4. We therefore grow up chasing a physical or sensual stimulus to quench the mental or spiritual needs our human being craves. Without thinking about it, due to our uneducated nature, our human being would translate every mental and spiritual notion or thought to fit our natural mind. Every *thing*, then, becomes our appetite, and becoming our appetite, we are moved to think on other ways to alleviate the negative sensation we put our own self through when over stimulating it, and through more flesh-based practices perceived to chain up that nature.

5. We truly are not born intelligent, and intelligent according to the living God's definition of intelligence, which definition is found in the saying, "Be renewed in the spirit of your mind,"[2] and, "That which is born of the Spirit is spirit."[3] Intelligence is understood through benevolence, and before one can be kind to another, they have to first be kind to their devotional self.

6. We see self's defect. We see the fault in the human being. We see the natural state of our person is not truly sober, but rather infected with a mind that is clearly not rational. The mission, then, for the human being, is to conquer its self by introducing into it a more complete stream of thought.

7. This introduction to a higher course of thought and feeling, being accomplished while the heart beats, is the challenge of being human. We are born ignorant of the other side of our humanity so that we can appreciate and respect others who have yet to know their challenge. By passing through the higher education of instructing self, we introduce our mind to the actual pain of feeling and thinking on the disappointment our words and actions can privately and publicly produce. Such a course of learning regenerates the heart to true sympathy for true empathy for those without this course of learning, allowing us to pass

---

2   Ephesians 4:23
3   John 3:6

through this life using our higher faculties for good, as opposed to the lower faculties for injury.

8. It is then good that we are not born with a full knowledge of good or of injury. Being established in both *arts*, we would consciously choose what is more natural, which can actually lead to the human being creating greater tragedies than when ignorant of "right" or "wrong." If born with a heart understanding its nature's code, it may seem that choosing "right" words and actions over "wrong" words and actions would occur, but the direction of our human being is naturally towards what feels good. If what feels good is the knowledge of injury, then that would be chosen, and who can say that that particular mind would ever care to shift their perspective, for they know both sides and have yet chosen what is preferred.

9. But we are born, and for good reason, ignorant of our nature's character. Being ignorant, we have the opportunity to receive unexpected correction, as opposed to being set in a direction where, due to comfort, correction is less likely to occur. With our faculties unmolested, the plague of an uneducated human nature doesn't now seem so deleterious, for that ignorance, with experience, only works to make us more kind to our self, and to every other mind encountering us.

10. Herein the will and wisdom of the living God is verified, for "the end of the commandment is charity out of a pure heart, and of a good conscience, and of faith unfeigned."[4]

11. It is evident that, being the Creator of the human nature, that Mind should provide a course of learning to better the human condition. This higher education is taught through the Creator's chief apostle suffering the tree who, "having abolished in his flesh the enmity, even the law of commandments contained in ordinances,"[5] pronounces *life's* key, that "the strength of sin is the law."[6]

12. The "flesh" nailed to the tree, or to the cross, represents a religious philosophy. To see that "flesh" crucified is to see that religious philosophy annihilated, becoming "sin" to entertain. It is therefore

---

4   1 Timothy 1:5
5   Ephesians 2:15
6   1 Corinthians 15:56

become "sin" to think, "You are justified by the law."[7] This revelation stands for both the natural and the devotional mind of the human being, but when first applied to the devotional, the condition of the natural will better.

13. Religious laws remove the conversation from view, causing the person to let what is handwritten think and feel for it. The person's *blessing* then, coming from what is handwritten, is liable to mislead their mind, hardening them to the doing of prescriptions above personally rationalizing for self's good. This, in turn, darkens the person's view of others, for if self is so engaged in a task for *righteousness*, how can it see how to lawfully treat another?

14. The doer of *creation's* new covenant science will therefore confess, "The law of the Spirit of life in Christ Jesus hath made me free from the law of sin and death."[8] Being liberated from the philosophy of the religious law, the conversation's conscience can freely think and feel on the Bible's words for the intended resurrection, even as it says, "Be ye transformed by the renewing of your mind, that ye may prove what is that good, and acceptable, and perfect, will of God."[9]

15. It would seem as though a transformation in doctrine wouldn't affect the person's kindness, but it will. Being knowledgeable of *creation's* science and an active participant of its prize, the heart becomes softer to others through the correction it has experienced.

16. Such a heart has learned of its particular nature, and of the injury it has caused, both to self and to other minds. It has seen the dark side of its mind, and warring with that mind to better its operation, it understands the struggle of introducing its conversation to a higher form of thought. This wisdom is what encourages it to be more sympathetic and empathetic towards others still unconscious to their own conversation's character, fulfilling the saying, "The end of the commandment is charity out of a pure heart, and of a good conscience, and of faith unfeigned."[10]

---

7   Galatians 5:4
8   Romans 8:2
9   Romans 12:2
10   1 Timothy 1:5

17. The human being is not naturally built to exercise true self-sacrificing love, but the living God's will and wisdom reveals that the human being is born to experience a course of learning contrary to its nature. When once the devotional mind is personally cultivated and established, such a mind can then educate its natural mind, as opposed to the natural mind controlling both physical and spiritual aspects of the human being. We are therefore born into the most beautiful experience, for we begin life empty in thought and in feeling, but we may conclude this life in reasonable benevolence.

18. This book introduces the reader to this benevolence, and to the course of learning whereby it is attained. Our conversation is to have a faith that works. Our faith is to have an expression revealing its Creator. By allowing our faith to develop, and through the intended form of learning, it can and will be, for both us and other minds, a working faith.

1

The Fruit of Longsuffering

1. "Make straight paths for your feet, lest that which is lame be turned out of the way,"[11] it is counseled, "but let it rather be healed. Follow peace with all men, and holiness, without which no man shall see the Lord."[12] "For though we walk in the flesh, we do not war after the flesh."[13] "Consider what I say,"[14] it says, "and the Lord give thee understanding in all things."[15]

2. Before any form of *peace* is considered, a diligent inquiry into how to care for our personal devotional character must first take place. Our faith's intellect is naturally sick and will never, of its own self, without embracing humility for a thorough re-education, see the

---

11   Hebrews 12:13
12   Hebrews 12:13,14
13   2 Corinthians 10:3
14   2 Timothy 2:7
15   2 Timothy 2:7

intention behind the Bible's philosophy in this condition. Our faith's re-education isn't meant to be depressing, but is to rather be uplifting due to the developing indwelling presence of the living God's will within our conversation's conscience. This course of learning is what adds *life* to our conversation.

3. The fruit of joy and peace will stimulate the growth of the fruit of longsuffering, for through us, we are to be an agent of health among broken minds. Surely, then, "the mouth of a righteous man is a well of life,"[16] and "a faithful ambassador is health."[17] This is why it says, ""Let them that love him be as the sun when he goeth forth in his might."[18]

4. The conversation cannot know the living God's will without first picking up a sincere spirit of sympathy and self-sacrificing love for its self. The mind cannot enter into the promised realm of understanding without first suffering internal philosophical warfare. "The husbandman that laboureth must be first partaker of the fruits,"[19] and if not, where then can a pleasant *tongue* be found? Our naturally fractured religious estate wars against the intention within the body of our spiritual understanding,"[20] and not one mind can be edified until it first manages the ground of its own belief.

5. If our conversation is not healed then it is surely diseased, and if it is damaged then what right do we have to endorse what is for a healthy conversation? Ought we not to discipline our own conversation?[21] The fruit of longsuffering is most needed if we are to contend for the Bible's devotional character, which is why it says, "The fruit of righteousness is sown in peace of them that make peace."[22]

6. Our joy and peace in the living God's wisdom means nothing if not outwardly expressed and honestly shared. While knowing the repercussions facing creation's survival and sufficiency, knowing that there

---

16   Proverbs 10:11
17   Proverbs 13:17
18   Judges 5:31
19   2 Timothy 2:7
20   Galatians 5:17
21   Romans 2:21
22   James 3:18

was a woe pronounced on the inhabitants of the *earth*, the living God, out of love, still permitted life to continue in a fractured habitation.

7. Without repeatedly demonstrating love throughout ecclesiastical history, bearing long with a negligent *people*, would we have a reason to look for a Creator that was mindful? Responsibility falls on us who profess the living God's *name*, which name, or devotional character, is self-sacrificing love first towards the conversation and then towards the human being. The sign of longsuffering is recognized through a love made available not by general or natural affection, but rather through the heart of action by reason, or through a "faith which worketh by love."[23] Should we then not endure our faith's chastening to qualify for such an impressive *fruit* as is longsuffering?

8. To endure injury through patience, to be slow to anger even through provocation, is to exemplify the inward workings of the knowledge of the living God's benevolence. The conversation possessing a character in likeness to the living God's devotional mind is gentle, striving to remain, to the end the heart of another may always come up in remembrance, conscious of the height and depth of that mind's kindness towards their self.

9. Although we don't know the complete position of another, or because we cannot truly comprehend the direction of another conversation, it doesn't mean that through impulse we cancel the living God's standards, compromising justification's new covenant principles because of our untrained temperament. This is why, for our instruction, the Bible's wisdom reveals, "The LORD is longsuffering, and of great mercy, forgiving iniquity and transgression, and by no means clearing the guilty, visiting the iniquity of the fathers upon the children unto the third and fourth generation."[24]

10. Again, "The LORD is merciful and gracious, slow to anger, and plenteous in mercy. He will not always chide: neither will he keep his anger forever."[25]

---

23   Galatians 5:6
24   Numbers 14:18
25   Psalms 103:8,9

11. And again, "Thou, O Lord, art a God full of compassion, and gracious, longsuffering, and plenteous in mercy and truth."[26]

12. Through the furnace of affliction, our faith is to personally endure chastening so that we would become familiar with our character defects, to the end we would repent of our devotional ignorance to receive inward correction, making our past comforts disgusting through having our errors manifested to our conscience. "I can of mine own self do nothing,"[27] said the living God's chief apostle, and it is no different for us, in that now, by the character of Bible's wisdom "we live, and move, and have our being."[28]

13. The living God's manner of love only seems heavy because of our natural *love* for what is contrary to it. Our personal faith, from its conception, is doesn't know an undefiled intelligent affection, yet the living God would not have us in this condition. Should minds caring to serve the living God not develop an uncomplaining and enduring spirit? The Bible's counsel is not distressing, but does lead to an increase in understanding.[29] Should we understand the man or the woman that our Creator sees in us, should we learn to remove pride from our heart, we would then mourn for our human condition, lamenting over our stubbornness to humbly magnify our Parent for bearing so long with us.

14. Just as the living God, being one that "will have compassion on us,"[30] accepts every sincere conversation approaching the Bible's wisdom, so too we must learn, from exercising self, to humble self when faced with a situation that is most aggravating. In every moment of despair and frustration, of anger or perplexity, we should seek to clearly do as through a fortified mind of reason. The same care that we perceive to be demonstrated by the living God towards us is the same gratuitous love we should reflect when faced with any manner of adversity, and we begin to reflect that manner of love when first embracing *creation's* course of learning.

---

26   Psalms 86:15
27   John 5:30
28   Acts 17:28
29   Proverbs 1:5
30   Micah 7:19

15. As students in the living God's classroom, we know that repentance is the key to receiving a blessing upon our faith's intellect. In agony we fall, in both shame and remorse, knowing that a violation of the Bible's confidence has been committed through either the weakness or the hardness of our heart. Not for our transgression, but rather for the relief of the weight of the action, we bend *heaven's* ear for forgiveness while knowing that we are not truly remorseful.

16. "Ye ask, and receive not, because ye ask amiss,"[31] it says. Yet, "I have purged thee,"[32] it is written, "and thou wast not purged."[33]

17. Has creation's *strength* failed? Has its wisdom lost power? No, but we are rather unbelieving that the words within the Bible can heal our thoughts and feelings. We are afraid of the experience to obtain personal and devotional wellbeing.

18. Nevertheless the living God responds with care, care that we who have not learned to exercise godly sorrow do overlook. The living God's commandment will not fail; that commandment's grace is full of power for the heart tired of slavery to self. The Bible's words will heal our sickness; they will encourage forgiveness within conversations deeply mourning their condition. Hereafter the conversation "shall not judge after the sight of his eyes, neither reprove after the hearing of his ears."[34]

19. To better remain apt to forgive, to constantly remember to remain sober and awake to the thoughts and feelings of another, we are first, while giving way for the growth of the spirit of our mind, to remain inwardly still. Our voice is heard, noted, and remembered; every tear and every word of edification is especially marked; this is why we are to never underestimate what another is going through.

20. We all experience the same joy and anguish.[35] To remember the conflicting relationship between the heart and the mind is to consider our self yet bonded to others that are torn by a contrary mind of oper-

31 James 4:3
32 Ezekiel 24:13
33 Ezekiel 24:13
34 Isaiah 11:3
35 2 Peter 5:9

ation. Though we may become aggravated, though we lack a pure understanding of surrounding circumstances, let it never be forgotten that we do desire the same treatment of equality from the same Creator, and are above nothing.

21. Where then is an excuse for any lack of effort to advance the Bible's standard of love? All are drowning in the same sorrow. Impatience will separate us from one another. For what reason do we uphold our profession without *fruit*? None are burdened when joined together in a right benevolent mind, for when the heart has pressed out its *wine*, fresh water is given for complete betterment.

2

Patience

1. Seeing that our faith is called to live out the mind of the Bible's philosophy, which mind is a conversation born out of love, or edification, due to exercising a practical application of its words, we have to remember that devotional sobriety is the Bible's ultimate intention.[36] The conversation should not feel ashamed to know or to execute the living God's standard. It does no good to compromise the principles of the Bible's philosophy. In so doing we remove peace from our faith's heart, relinquishing the precious treasures from the journey of our devotional experience.

2. Strengthened by the wisdom acquired from the Bible, and remaining grateful toward our Father for that rare experience,[37] let us maintain our confidence as creations of the living God.[38] While

---

36   2 Timothy 1:7,8
37   Colossians 1:11,12
38   Philippians 2:15

"holding forth the word of life,"[39] let us be a fair example of the beauty of *holiness* that we may confess: "I have not run in vain, neither labored in vain."[40]

3. Submitting our conversation to the living God's will and wisdom allows us to confidently enter all situations knowing that our exit has already been established from how we enter into them. While aware of that wisdom's presence and remaining patient in heart and in mind, our every word, our every action, our thoughts and emotions, should stem from the good work of patience that is prescribed for our experience. Our faith will not be complete without relinquishing its intellect to the living God's science. Failing to do so will result in our conversation either blessing or cursing a heart that would know the sufficiency of its instruction.

4. Our conversation is to be "an habitation of God through the Spirit,"[41] being established by the living God's course of learning. Should we, for one moment, wrongly represent the character of this wisdom, we will hurt our own heart, and to another make ugly *creation's* experience. Yet our mind is welcomed into the Bible's intention for a reason, and in much longsuffering its words will refine us. Should we then not remain patient with another, or even with our own self? This is why it says that with patience, the good ground, after honestly hearing and keeping the words, inwardly benefited.[42]

5. The living God bears long with us through our degenerate devotional state because it is to see, at the time appointed, intended love. To work under our own *power* without being invigorated by the living God's wisdom proves our religion to be a false religion. We are to experience because we are to learn, and from learning we are to do, and from doing we are to understand the importance of committing self to the knowledge obtained that from a, "Thus saith," care in an inexpressible fashion is made plain to the heart hardened by traditional debauchery. Do we then dare to ignore the importance of incorporating

---

39   Philippians 2:16
40   Philippians 2:16
41   Ephesians 2:22
42   Luke 8:15

a longsuffering spirit into our character, and without diligently adding to it a patient character?

6. Should one have the courage to endure excruciating situations and "offend not in word, the same is a perfect man, and able also to bridle the whole body."[43] Only by depending on the knowledge gained when exercising faith on the living God's words can we ever come to value the very breath in our lungs. Despite what we go through, the living God understands who and what we are."[44]

7. Should we incline our heart to retain wisdom, we will learn the living God's *fear*, from that *fear* we will withdraw from religious error to grow more fervent in mind for a right manner of devotion. Though our faith is naturally conceived in religious error, the living God has not, nor will ever, quit the conversation counting on the Bible's *voice* for counsel. We are counted worthy to presently suffer for knowledge of *creation's* standard, and seeing that we succeed by acknowledging that every victory is won by the strength contained with the Bible's words, let us never doubt, or feel shame, because of our present personal or devotional condition.

8. Patience, when cultivated, ensures that our personal and devotional conversation remains intelligent, honest, and immaculate.[45] Should we correctly examine the Bible, we will find that every illustration within it is but a proverb detailing why it is important to develop patience.[46] The living God, for their benefit, put every faithful conversation in harm,[47] never forgetting them. This was done so that we may know "that the Lord is very pitiful, and of tender mercy."[48]

9. Patience will perfect the thoughts and feelings of our conversation. If patience should settle into the experience, it would help blossom and bud the fruit of longsuffering. The exercising of patience is a joy because we know that every trial will bring knowledge of the

---

43   James 3:2
44   Psalms 103:13,14
45   James 1:2-4
46   James 5:10,11
47   Hebrews 11:38
48   James 5:11

intended experience.[49] The living God will not keep our confidence in the torment of a broken mind or heart, but will eventually alleviate it.[50] This is why we are to earn wisdom by patiently handling our self, and why it says, "Wisdom is profitable to direct."[51]

10. Every trial that we encounter is to be an advancing step in our conversation's purification.[52] A longsuffering spirit may be joined to us if we will for it. This is why it also says, "For whom the Lord loveth he chasteneth, and scourgeth every son whom he receiveth. If ye endure chastening, God dealeth with you as with sons; for what son is he whom the father chasteneth not? But if ye be without chastisement, whereof all are partakers, then are ye bastards, and not sons."[53]

11. Knowledge on how to regulate self is to be delivered to us when patiently disciplining our conversation, which is why patience is that principle making our conversation's conscience perfect. When adding this work to that spirit of longsuffering, enduring even at the cost of the heart's provocation, surely we will, both within and without, be able to do a right work alongside the Bible's philosophy. When it comes time to have our faith measured in the *fire* of affliction, let us then remember how it says, "Do well, and suffer for it, ye take it patiently."[54] This is why, when in *creation's* classroom, we are to commit our faith to the living God's words.[55]

12. To suffer for the Bible's present will is nothing less than suffering for the purpose of a right personal and devotional character. Built up through conflict that we would develop a greater and yet bolder respect for the living God's precious and peculiar love, our education is to be the living God's benevolence quickening the devotional mind from unhealthy natural and religious passions to confess, "Man doth not live

---

49   Psalms 16:11
50   1 Corinthians 10:13
51   Ecclesiastes 10:10
52   2 Corinthians 12:9
53   Hebrews 12:6-8
54   1 Peter 2:20
55   1 Peter 4:19

by bread only, but by every word that proceedeth out of the mouth of the LORD."[56]

13. The end of patience is the living God's mind of devotion dwelling within our conversation's conscience. Can there be any higher honor or privilege given to our faith? Through patience, the living God's wisdom will ensure our faith's perfection by grace, so how much more favorable is it to be longsuffering towards another who wants that same joy? This is why it says, "We desire that every one of you do shew the same diligence to the full assurance of hope unto the end,"[57] and, "Be not slothful, but followers of them who through faith and patience inherit the promises."[58]

14. The hope of the living God's *glory* or kindness resting within our inward person is that good hope strengthening our mind as we bear long in affliction. With every unfavorable circumstance, should we endure with a right attitude, comes the opportunity to have the knowledge of a right affection embedded within our inward person.[59]

15. To possess the Bible's philosophy is not enough unless we personally acknowledge it, and to acknowledge the Bible's philosophy is not enough unless we actively keep it. Intellectually and spiritually we are to digest its words that they may be practically experienced. Hereafter may the reception of grace increase our knowledge in the living God's science.[60] Hereafter it may be fulfilled, "That my joy may remain in you, and that your joy might be full."[61]

16. It is written, "Israel hath cast off the thing that is good,"[62] yet we are counseled, "That good thing which was committed unto thee keep by the Holy Ghost which dwelleth in us."[63] That "good thing" is the living God's wisdom, teaching us that compassion mingled with self-sacrifice is needed if we would retain *creation's* present blessing.

---

56   Deuteronomy 8:3
57   Hebrews 6:11
58   Hebrews 6:12
59   John 14:21
60   2 Peter 3:18
61   John 15:11
62   Hosea 8:3
63   2 Timothy 1:14

What, then, is needed in order to make that wisdom our main diet? It says, "Greater love hath no man than this, that a man lay down his life for his friends."[64]

17. The development of patience, through the work of mental and inward anguish, is to give way to the conviction of the heart and to the conversion of the mind. Only by experiencing grief can we come to respect and reverence the living God's patience and longsuffering for our faith's cultivation. From understanding such temperance, we will stand in awe at the thought of how mercy can excel knowledge. We will open our hearts to the admiration of the only true and living God, allowing our person to willingly embrace its blessing through doing for another what is done for it. Let it then be that, for "the race that is set before us,"[65] we "follow after righteousness, godliness, faith, love, patience, meekness."[66]

---

64   John 15:13
65   Hebrews 12:1
66   1 Timothy 6:11

3

Be Still

1. "After he had washed their feet, and had taken his garments, and was set down again, he said unto them, Know ye what I have done to you?"[67]

2. The first disciples received the greatest commandment through this service. Through this *ordinance*, the living God's chief apostle utters the foundation of his doctrine's law, stating, "Use not liberty for an occasion to the flesh, but by love serve one another."[68] Thus, "I have given you an example,"[69] he says, "that ye should do as I have done unto you."[70]

3. The first thing done for the disciples was not the washing of their feet, but rather he "laid aside his garments; and took a towel, and girded

---

67   John 13:12
68   Galatians 5:13
69   John 13:15
70   John 13:15

himself."[71] This man put aside his flesh's covering, or his own heart's covering, and took to covering and wrapping his self with a linen cloth.

4. In another place it is written that one "begged the body of Jesus,"[72] and when it was delivered to him, he took the body and "wrapped it in a clean linen cloth. And laid it in his own new tomb."[73] This Rabbi's first act was not to wash the feet of the disciples. Before commencing, he gave them an example of how necessary it is for even him to have laid his own conversation to *death*, wrapping himself with a *garment* of knowledgeable self-sacrifice that he may perfectly and decently render his service.

5. "Whosoever will be great among you, shall be your minister,"[74] this same man says, "and whosoever of you will be the chiefest, shall be servant of all."[75] Herein it is that "love is the fulfilling of the law,"[76] for it is written, "If ye know these things, happy are ye if ye do them."[77] This is why it says, "He that keepeth the law, happy is he,"[78] and, "If ye keep my commandments, ye shall abide in my love; even as I have kept my Father's commandments, and abide in his love."[79]

6. By practicing how to humble the heart, by subduing our natural and devotional thoughts and imaginations, we will care to consistently live with the doctrine the living God's chief minister taught, which doctrine, in order that we may better keep and faithfully fulfill *creation's* course, rests in the joy of humbling our conversation for the benefit of another. This doctrine, when exercised within the life, states, "Ye also ought to wash one another's feet,"[80] proving that our experience has been with the living God's science, and that its devotional character is

---

71   John 13:4
72   Matthew 27:58
73   Matthew 27:59,60
74   Matthew 10:43
75   Matthew 10:44
76   Romans 13:10
77   John 13:17
78   Proverbs 29:18
79   John 15:10
80   John 13:14

the guide of our experience. This is why it says: "By this shall all men know that ye are my disciples, if ye have love one to another."[81]

7. It is for us to observe the conversation that "laid down his life for us,"[82] who came "to give his life a ransom for many,"[83] that we in turn may suffer our conversation to be re-educated for learning how "we ought to lay down our lives."[84] As creations of the living God's words, we are counseled, "Present your bodies a living sacrifice,"[85] to the end that "every one of us please his neighbor for his good to edification."[86] "These things have I spoken unto you, that my joy might remain in you,"[87] says the living God's wisdom.

8. Creation's chief minister enjoyed keeping the living God's commandments. This man would have us keep his Father's commandments through his doctrine to rest in his conversation's joy. By learning to love as he did, we may then rest in his labor of love to better keep his Father's commandments also, even as it is written, "That they might have my joy fulfilled in themselves."[88]

9. His doctrine is the means whereby the wonderful will of the living God may be given absolute consent to be written on our heart. "Wash you, make you clean,"[89] says this man's philosophy. "Put away"[90] and "learn to do well,"[91] it advises.

10. We learn how to do well from hearing, keeping, applying and then proving the Bible's words in our lives. From relieving one another after we have allowed self to fall short of its intention, we display an unselfish disposition through service to one another, upholding the Bible's manner of love. Indeed we through our actions are a living

---

81   John 13:35
82   1 John 3:16
83   Mark 10:45
84   1 John 3:16
85   Romans 12:1
86   Romans 15:2
87   John 15:11
88   John 17:13
89   Isaiah 1:16
90   Isaiah 1:16
91   Isaiah 1:16

testimony to the fact that the living God's will is the greatest liberty to exercise.

11. If we would dare treat the wounds of another, it is that we must first "learn to shew piety at home,"[92] within. This is why it says, "What? Know ye not that your body is the temple of the Holy Ghost which is in you, which ye have of God, and ye are not your own?"[93]

12. It is no surprise that we first have an inward temple to cleanse, for the household within our heart, our good and our bad *children* we have brought up from a youth, need to be subdued and corrected. The doer of the living God's science must then be "one that ruleth well his own house, having his children in subjection with all gravity."[94] To set the example, one must "take heed to thyself,"[95] "for in so doing thou shalt both save thyself, and them that hear thee,"[96] as it is written, "In me first Jesus Christ might shew forth all longsuffering, for a pattern to them which should hereafter believe."[97]

13. The living God's chief apostle has given us an example to practice. If this man first put away his garments before he could wash the feet of his disciples, so too we must heed the command, "Set thine house in order,"[98] if we would justly handle, and with a self-sacrificing heart, the burdens of one another. "Whom the LORD loveth he correcteth,"[99] therefore it is necessary to first correct the *sons* and *daughters* of our own *house*, which is why it says, "Correct thy son, and he shall give thee rest; yea, he shall give delight unto thy soul."[100]

14. "A man's foes shall be they of his own household,"[101] and the conversation desiring the crown of *life* needs to pick up a war against its own self, learning to positively aggravate those prevailing dispositions

---

92   1 Timothy 5:4
93   1 Corinthians 6:19
94   1 Timothy 3:4
95   1 Timothy 4:16
96   1 Timothy 4:16
97   1 Timothy 1:16
98   Isaiah 38:1
99   Proverbs 3:12
100   Proverbs 29:17
101   Matthew 10:36

that will cause us to miss the intended refreshing. The Bible is calling every mind desiring personal knowledge of its *name* to first become diligent learners. Without an active experience and a living education on its present philosophy, the heart will grow numb to the movement of its intention.

15. To be a learner in the Bible's classroom means to allow the Bible to have an entrance into our heart that it may be exercised in the life. "A reproof entereth more into a wise man"[102] because "he that hath knowledge spareth his words."[103] "The Lord GOD hath given me the tongue of the learned,"[104] declares the wise, because that wisdom "hath opened mine ear, and I was not rebellious, neither turned away back."[105] If we would "know how to speak a word in season to him that is weary,"[106] then as it is written, we must first open our ears, departing, regardless of known or unknown consequences, from natural traditional inclinations to endure the Bible's counsel, even as it is says, "Be still, and know that I am God."[107]

16. A personal duty rests on the conversation professing the Bible's *name* to know the *name* of its chief apostle and the standard of that *name's* experience. When once we learn to do well, opening our ear to the living God's counsel, then may we do well, opening ears by the wise counsel given to us from our experience. This is why it says, "Even as our beloved brother Paul also according to the wisdom given unto him,"[108] and, "I caused the widow's heart to sing for joy."[109] Hereafter may we prove how "God resisteth the proud, and giveth grace to the humble."[110]

17. "Whosoever of you will be the chiefest, shall be servant of all";[111] this is the foundation of true education. Lessons learned that are

---

102   Proverbs 17:10
103   Proverbs 17:27
104   Isaiah 50:4
105   Isaiah 50:5
106   Isaiah 50:4
107   Psalms 46:10
108   2 Peter 3:15
109   Job 29:13
110   1 Peter 5:5
111   Mark 10:44

heard and never advanced, they are in vain spoken because the heart, "not being mixed with faith,"[112] refuses to support the thought. A "faith which worketh by love"[113] gives birth to "a new creature"[114] because by service the heart is encouraged to remain sanctified in its under-standing. This is why *creation's* discipline edifies,[115] and why its wisdom is given to the conversation consistently developing its character.[116]

18. Our greatest mistake is in allowing our mind to unlawfully high-light our deficiencies. Our greatest error is in allowing our heart to convince us that our shame has brought us into horrible standings with the Creator, therefore we cannot approach *heaven*. These feelings are contrary to the Bible's counsel. The Bible would have us enter into council with it over the trouble we have in disciplining our self. Before we can grasp any of its words, we must first lay hold of our *tongue*, casting away the cruel garment that is around our heart to remember the living God's undying care for our inward health.

19. In silence we must hear the Bible's words and let them pass through the heavily guarded domain of the *palace*, and as we guide every word into the inner courts of our *kingdom*, the entrance of that counsel will, as its wisdom begins to purge our *floors* of rubbish, imbue new life. The effect of silencing the thoughts or opinions concerning this *thing* or *that*, and simply doing the counsel to add wisdom by faith, will create "a perfect man,"[117] and one "able also to bridle the whole body."[118]

20. Wisdom cannot be separated from prudence, for it is careful and circumspect thoughts that are the life of the conscience. Reproof cannot be separated from wisdom, for it is from experiencing the Bible's philosophy that *life* is added to the soul, and wise counsel and understanding given to the careful observer. Discretion cannot also be separated from obedience. By developing power over the will so that the *tongue* is kept and guarded, the appetite, along with its inclinations

---

112   Hebrews 4:2
113   Galatians 5:6
114   Galatians 6:15
115   Romans 8:2
116   Romans 8:4
117   James 3:2
118   James 3:2

and passions, is given to reason over the living God's words to blossom and bud newness of *life*. Learning to subdue self is a great and healthful work that trains the mind to remain content. Daily the heart must be trained to remain in silence that its condition receives health from the wisdom developing within it.

21. The living God requires us to be learners who subdue temperament for the sake of better retaining knowledge to free our conscience. We are to break our hearts at the sight of our condition and to then uplift our will to be healed. We are to re-educate our conversation and not sacrifice our individuality. The goal is to live in the living God's devotional mind from personally encountering the Bible's counsel to honor that counsel not through the body, but through the mind.[119]

22. "What hath the wise more than the fool? What hath the poor, that knoweth to walk before the living?"[120] "The heart of the wise is in the house of mourning; but the heart of fools is in the house of mirth."[121]

23. Our faith's *household* needs to get set in order by a living experience. Silence is eloquence, and by reflecting on self, by allowing the Bible's words into the soul, our personal and devotional infirmities will then take so strong of a hold on us that we will not want to move away from its wisdom. When the heart receives the living God's intention and decides to apply it at all costs, the instruction learned will add godly fear and wise counsel to the lips and to the mind.

24. The Bible's wisdom declares that developing a heart for service towards its understanding is our conversation's lifework. Our conversation is to be created in the image of its devotional character from the moment it accepts its wisdom as personal Savior. A personal devotional experience cannot be avoided without the Creator's hands perfecting our conversation, for by a living education in *things* higher than the sight and tied to the trying of the mind, we may have a sure journey individually, and yet equally.

---

119   Philippians 3:3
120   Ecclesiastes 6:8
121   Ecclesiastes 7:4

4

The Life of Our Hand

1. "Only ye shall not eat the blood; ye shall pour it upon the earth as water."[122]

2. As a memorial to celebrate the good that *God* had given, anciently, Israel was invited, that *God* my joy in them and they in *Him*, to bring their *household*, along with their offerings, sacrifices, tithes, and vows to honor the name of the *God* who had honored them. Yet they were counseled, before eating, because "the life of the flesh is in the blood,"[123] to first put away the blood.

3. The blood of the sacrifice, in addition to being used as a vehicle to drive guilt home, represented a fortified conversation apart from religious error. The shedding of the blood was to symbolize to their mind that "almost all things are by the law purged with blood; and

---

122   Deuteronomy 12:16
123   Leviticus 17:11

20

without shedding of blood is no remission."[124] Through the spilling of blood is the purging of a supposedly filthy personal and devotional conscience, yet to eat the blood of the sacrifice represented an impure offering, showing that the stain of *sin* on the mind was not completely acknowledged as being removed, but was still secretly cherished.

4. As with ancient Israel, those within modern *Israel* are to not presently eat the *flesh* with the *blood*. We are counseled not to do so for an important reason.

5. "Thou art wearied in the greatness of thy way," it is written of the halfhearted, "yet saidst thou not, There is no hope: thou hast found the life of thine hand; therefore thou wast not grieved."[125]

6. The "life" that has become our "hand," or our dedicated *thing* of obedience, is that error committed through the absence of possessing the living God's *name* within the heart. This "life," due to its comfort, is that philosophical error we consent to. Though we ask for forgiveness, sincerely wanting to be freed from this burden preventing us from knowing *creation's* science, we carry unbelief in what we ask for and do not believe that forgiveness and pardon are given. We lead an experience where wrong is repeated, and where we only know an up and down negative and stressful energy.

7. *Blindness* is imparted to our conversation mostly because the living God can discern its heart, in that "they did not like to retain God in their knowledge."[126] Knowing that this or that conversation asks faithlessly, or out of pride and envy, devotional blindness is given because it would use the blessing either carelessly or for oppression.

8. It is written, "If any of you lack wisdom, let him ask of God...let him ask in faith, nothing wavering. For he that wavereth is like a wave of the sea driven with the wind and tossed. For let not that man think that he shall receive any thing of the Lord."[127]

---

124   Hebrews 9:22
125   Isaiah 57:10
126   Romans 1:28
127   James 1:5-7

9. "Whatever ye shall ask in my name, that will I do,"[128] says the Bible's wisdom, yet to ask while carrying unbelief, to ask while consciously living off of the *blood*, or the "life," of our religious error, we ask in vain through an unbelieving heart. But rather know that "this is the confidence that we have in him, that, if we ask any thing according to his will, he heareth us: and if we know that he hear us, whatsoever we ask, we know that we have the petitions that we desire of."[129]

10. "Woe to them that devise iniquity, and work evil upon their beds!"[130] we read. "When morning is light, they practise it, because it is in the power of their hand."[131]

11. Because past habitual tendencies are comforting, philosophical error continues in the personal and devotional life because there is no effort to allow the living God's wisdom to rewrite the heart's pattern. Many "weary themselves to commit iniquity"[132] because if they should have believed in the power of the living God's words to remove error the first time, there would be no need to later commit the same error again. Presently the living God's wisdom says to its professed believer, "In thy filthiness is lewdness: because I have purged thee, and thou wast not purged."[133]

12. Only through self-denial and self-regulation can the conversation receive health. The conversation that "hath forgotten that he was purged from his old sins"[134] continues therein, wearying its heart and growing heavier in mind because it fights an experience desiring to write advice within it. To eat the "life," or to eat the *blood* of such a *sacrifice* will only keep the heart against the character of that experience's wisdom. It is this wisdom written on our heart, and in our mind, that places us in perfect harmony with the living God's devotional character.

---

128 John 14:3
129 1 John 5:14,15
130 Micah 2:1,2
131 Micah 2:1,2
132 Jeremiah 9:5
133 Ezekiel 24:13
134 2 Peter 1:9

13. "Have ye not asked them that go by the way? And do ye not know their tokens, that the wicked is reserved to the day of destruction?"[135] it is written in the book of Job. "They shall be brought forth to the day of wrath."[136] "Hast thou marked the old way which the wicked men have trodden?"[137]

14. As the erroneous conversation takes its journey into injury, saying to the living God's science, "Depart from us: and what can the Almighty do,"[138] the students of that science are to cease from eating their own *flesh* to settle upon the *flesh* and *blood* of that science's understanding. The "flesh" referenced is not the literal flesh, but is the "body" of belief. The *flesh* of the Bible's understanding is to be eaten; our conversation cannot eat the Bible's philosophy while also feasting on the "life" or the pride of our devotional error.[139]

15. The erroneous conversation will continue in its "life" and will fail to sacrifice it upon the altar of *creation's* science. The *blood* of that science's wisdom is the only blood that we are to consume, even as it says, "I am the resurrection, and the life."[140] To eat the *flesh* of the living God's chief apostle means to entrust the conversation's conscience to his spiritual understanding, to partake of both the joy and the suffering of that understanding's experience.[141]

16. The *flesh* and the "life" of our *sacrifice* cannot be consumed together, for the blood of the sacrifice, which atones for our devotional wretchedness, is to be poured out to the living God's wisdom and removed from our heart that it may dwell within our faith's thoughts and feelings. This wisdom is *life*, and in its *flesh* is life, and in its *blood* is cleanliness atoning from religious error, therefore if we are to eat the *flesh*, or the conversation of the living God's chief minister, yet consume the "life" of our *hand* at the same time, we understand that our religion is false, our efforts are in vain, and we are yet deceiving our self.

---

135   Job 21:29,30
136   Job 21:30
137   Job 22:15
138   Job 22:17
139   Colossians 2:11
140   John 11:25
141   John 6:57

17. Through unfeigned love, and joy for the hope of a healthy devotional mind, we are to willingly afflict our conversation. Out of gratuitous love for the living God's *sacrifice*, our conversation must desire "to be found in him."[142] To become acquainted with the life and sufferings of this minister, and to even assimilate our own conversation with his, to yet drink the "life" of the *body* of our naturally erroneous conversation, we keep our faith's character backsliding.

18. We cannot honor the Bible's philosophy, praising it for the good that it has supposedly completed in our life, if we cease to allow its wisdom to fully place its right devotional character within our conversation's conscience. When doing anything for the living God, should the "life" of our *hand* stay close to our heart, our devotion is not completely pure.

19. If we desire our conversation to be a disciple of *creation's* present science, the "life" of our *hand* must quit its natural devotional understanding. This is why it says, "If any man come to me, and hate not his father, and mother, and wife, and children, and brethren, and sisters, yea, and his own life also, he cannot be my disciple."[143]

20. The "life" we are to hate is that conversation having no experience with the living God's words. If this "life" is not hated, how then can we love and accept the living God in full? This is why it says, "He that findeth his life shall lose it,"[144] and, He that loseth his life for my sake shall find it."[145]

21. Losing that naturally reproachful conversation ensures us the living God's present blessing. To properly know and execute the Bible's wisdom, the erroneous religious mind must be forgotten; this is why it says, "Put off concerning the former conversation the old man...and be renewed in the spirit of your mind."[146] If sacrificed, and if sacrificed through painstaking efforts to tax the mind to discover the living God's knowledge, we will be created free from the weight we so ignorantly carry.

---

142   Philippians 3:9
143   Luke 14:26
144   Matthew 10:39
145   Matthew 10:39
146   Ephesians 4:22,23

5

Enduring in Him

1. The "him" is, in right context of language, the living God's wisdom. The conversation abiding by that wisdom's manner of love will never be without showers of blessing upon the garden of their heart. The conversation cannot enter into its intended experience without first suffering its mind to be troubled by the living God's words. No conversation will know the present dispensation of the Bible's benevolence without first submitting to the requirements of that benevolence. How, then, can we expect to remain confident in the Bible's intention without first exercising self to know its will?

2. "The remnant of Israel shall not do iniquity, nor speak lies; neither shall a deceitful tongue be found in their mouth,"[147] so for what reason do we falsely lower *creation's* standard instead of magnifying it? Blessed is the conversation seeing the need to remain loyal to the living

---

147   Zephaniah 3:13

God's wisdom for sustenance; only then can it know that the true and living God is a healing wisdom[148] that "retaineth not his anger for ever, because he delighteth in mercy."[149]

3. To endure in the living God's wisdom, maintaining a good heart and a sober mind through present difficulties, is to show forth the inward work of faith and love outwardly. Should we lack that *gold* tried in the *fire* then our conversation will not receive that *raiment* to cover its shame, and should we lack that *gold* then we are not qualified to receive that *eye salve* to see our faith's condition. A stubborn disposition to continue in religious ignorance only expresses the true revelation of the experience; no conversation will receive the blessing of a new heart through an unlawfully self-sufficient spirit.

4. Yet the penitent will confess, "I acknowledge my transgression: and my sin is ever before me."[150] These will then hear, "Turn ye even to me with all your heart, and with fasting, and with weeping, and with mourning, and rend your heart, and not your garments, and turn unto the LORD your God."[151] They will hear how it says, "I will forgive their iniquity, and I will remember their sin no more,"[152] and, "He is gracious and merciful, slow to anger, and of great kindness, and repenteth him of the evil."[153]

5. Our conversation cannot receive pardon unless our heart is willingly and consensually broken at the sight and knowledge of its condition, and if there is a fight against that revelation, we fight against the only experience bettering our human condition. Devotional health takes time to capture, in the same sense that a wound over time comes to simply resemble a scar. Our faith is scarred from *birth* with a trait surpassing any genetic error; the only remedy is to follow the requirements necessary for the best possible recovery.

---

148   Micah 7:18
149   Micah 7:18
150   Psalms 51:3
151   Joel 2:13
152   Jeremiah 31:34
153   Joel 2:13

6. The living God's wisdom has determined that its student receive a wound to their heart for purifying their personal and devotional character. "For your patience and faith in all your persecutions and tribulations that ye endure,"[154] know that it is a sign that you are seen as being worthy to enter in to and then to graduate from the living God's course of learning.[155] This is why it says, "Whosoever doth not bear his cross, and come after me, cannot be my disciple."[156]

7. To mourn before the living God is not to quit life, professing the experience to be that of a depressing burden above a blessing. Our mourning is not a mourning tending to natural sorrow, but by "esteeming the reproach of Christ greater riches than the treasures of Egypt,"[157] we secure knowledge of our living experience. To "have respect unto the recompense of the reward"[158] cannot be done contrary to the directions given. The living God is a wisdom of principle, and the conversation seeking to be its subject needs to embrace its principles over its natural devotional perception.

8. Should we now not submit to *his* free remedy, how then can we expect to know the intended refreshing? Remember Abraham, who "after he had patiently endured, he obtained the promise."[159] And remember Moses, how "he forsook Egypt, not fearing the wrath of the king: for he endured, as seeing him who is invisible."[160] "Whatsoever things were written aforetime were written for our learning, that we through patience and comfort of the scriptures might have hope";[161] yet, "He that feareth is not made perfect in love."[162]

9. "There is no fear in love; but perfect love casteth out fear";[163] yet there is a fear, as a wall wearing religious error and lies, around the

---

154   2 Thessalonians 1:4
155   2 Thessalonians 1:5
156   Luke 14:27
157   Hebrews 11:26
158   Hebrews 11:26
159   Hebrews 6:15
160   Hebrews 11:27
161   Romans 15:4
162   1 John 4:18
163   1 John 4:18

heart of the conversation claiming to stand under *creation's* banner. Because of fear, wounds of affliction are seen as incurable and the experience of the living God's words is slighted. There is a shout of *health*, there is a joy of *wisdom*, and *life* is breathed into the mind of many, yet living corpses are in our midst. So think: of what force is your "awakening" attributed to? The devotional character will match its experience, and the experience will reflect what spirit has been accepted to lead its course.

10. The heart of experimental rebellion is comfortably situated where there is a cherished fear. The definition of the living God's devotional character is benevolence; godly fear doesn't stop devotional growth.[164] "Wherefore we receiving a kingdom which cannot be moved, let us have grace, whereby we may serve God acceptably with reverence and godly fear,"[165] remembering that "he that covereth his sins shall not prosper: but whoso confesseth and forsaketh them shall have mercy."[166]

11. We should aim for the experience given by the living God's wisdom. Our conversation does not, according to its natural affiliation with the religious world, know what it ought to honor, the end of that profession being the deterioration of its love and *body*. What more does the living God ask of us who profess to love *him* but to honor the Bible's wisdom, magnify that wisdom's kindness in our life, and consent to its showers of blessing upon our thoughts and feelings?

12. Love is not demonstrated in sporadic periods of expression. Love is not restrained by fear. The Bible's counsels are not oppressive. The process of justification is never so burdensome that we need to rest in our own thinking. Herein is why it says, "To this man will I look, even to him that is poor and of a contrite spirit, and trembleth at my words."[167]

13. If we believe it is impossible to comprehend the Bible's words, and to even practically reproduce them, then for what reason do we

---

164   2 Corinthians 7:10
165   Hebrews 12:28
166   Proverbs 28:13
167   Isaiah 66:2

frustrate our self? Doesn't it say, "Grieve not the holy Spirit of God"?[168] If we would believe so negatively about *creation's* experience, then for what reason do we drown in an obscure understanding of our profession? We are made to suffer for wisdom's reproach to build up hope through enduring in its promised intention. Not only is our conversation to be edified, but also our bond to our Creator.

14. Because it is the Bible's wisdom that will heal our devotional mind, though we are counted worthy to suffer for its *name* for a season, we will not be left to a contrary will, or even to the misleading impressions of our heart, but will be sealed with that necessary revelation of its *voice*. Our conversation, through the knowledge of the Bible's philosophy, is to grow and develop *fruit*; the conversation submitting to such an education must first personally learn of and prove the knowledge they acquire through trial and error.

---

168 Ephesians 4:30

6

The Way of Holiness

1. Says the prophet, "An highway shall be there, and a way, and it shall be called the way of holiness; the unclean shall not pass over it; but it shall be for those: the wayfaring men, though fools, shall not err therein."[169]

2. Because the unclean conversation cannot learn practical godliness, which is a practical devotional diet to arrive at and exercise the knowledge of the Bible's kindness, it is of necessity that it learns the *way* of *holiness*. This practice leading to the conversation's perfection involves a *highway*, or a course of learning, and the way of holiness begins with consent to allow the living God to write *creation's* doctrine on our heart, the end being to "condescend to men of low estate,"[170]

---

169   Isaiah 35:8
170   Romans 12:16

even like as it says, "For as the sufferings of Christ abound in us, so our consolation also aboundeth by Christ."[171]

3. This *highway* is made through the foundation of the Bible's science, which science is taught through the illustration of the living God's chief apostle suspended between heaven and earth. With that science as our diet, alleviation will appear to our conversation's conscience.[172] Hereafter, by immersing self in this course of learning, our conversation joins into that *assembly* honoring the living God's *name*, and for the purpose of being trained to be a blessing to others.[173]

4. Our conversation finds new life through the living God's wisdom or finds, through that science, a recovering devotional mind and character, which is why it says, "The highway of the upright is to depart from evil: he that keepeth his way preserveth his soul."[174] Though many "leave the paths of uprightness, to walk in the ways of darkness,"[175] they who understand that the *way* is narrow and for a reflection leading to the joy of a free devotional heart and conscience will "put on the new man, which is renewed in knowledge after the image of him that created him."[176]

5. Our conversation, through salvation's science, is to be sealed within walls of *peace*, removing from every contrary religious principle so it may know that "the love of Christ, which passeth knowledge,"[177] is knowledge of devotional wellbeing. We are to sit with this science to daily learn about the government it endorses so that we may be found worthy to experience it. Through this process our conversation is to work with *him* to remove our personal and devotional character defects, but for its character to exist within our conversation's conscience, we need to mentally commit to consistent consecration. This is why it says, "Let us cleanse ourselves from all filthiness of the flesh and spirit, perfecting holiness in the fear of God."

---

171   2 Corinthians 1:5
172   Romans 10:13
173   1 John 3:23
174   Proverbs 16:17
175   Proverbs 2:13
176   Colossians 3:10
177   Ephesians 3:19

6. To be *holy* means to justly present and maintain the conversation through the living God's wisdom. It is to live up to the measure of the living God's standard devotional character in our sphere through the force of *his* words. The conversation willingly consenting to this course of learning, returning the blessing obtained upon hearts around it and perfecting the character of that wisdom through patiently doing well, retains a greater knowledge of its self to further its consecration.

7. Through consecration to the living God's wisdom we dedicate our conversation's members to the inward work of that wisdom, for it is written, "Let not sin therefore reign in your mortal body."[178] A practical application of godliness is then consecration and dedication of self to the living God's mind. Only conversations yielding their self to the labor of that *Mind* can travel to that *Place* of *rest*. This is why the Bible stresses personal devotional consecration.[179] A blessing is upon the conversation personally taking their *cross*, or their faith's defect, upon their shoulder to let the instruction of the living God's mind heal it.

8. It is written, "If so be that ye have heard him, and have been taught by him, as the truth is in Jesus: that ye put off concerning the former conversation the old man, which is corrupt according to the deceitful lusts; and be renewed in the spirit of your mind. And that ye put on the new man, which after God is created in righteousness and true holiness."[180]

9. The intended experience of devotional creation is a bitter battle between the mind within the natural and the devotional body, and the spirit of the mind within the inward person, yet we are counseled to personally read and study the scriptures.[181] By seeking knowledge of practical godliness from out of the Bible, which "godliness" is practical devotional order, our conversation will not seek after its former mate, or its old devotional mind. No conversation desiring knowledge of how to possess the intended mind of devotion will fail of a love that is necessary for reflecting the *image* of that knowledge.

---

178   Romans 6:12
179   Exodus 32:29
180   Ephesians 4:20-24
181   Isaiah 34:16

10. Because its philosophies are contrary to the living God's devotional character, our old devotional mind cannot lead us to experience the living God's will. By refusing to entertain self-cultivated and inherited notions on what that devotional character is honoring, when the new mind of devotion is exercised, our conversation will rightly seek wellbeing, enjoying its search for the living God's manner of righteousness to claim true holiness. This is why our faith must know "that our old man is crucified with him, that the body of sin might be destroyed."[182]

11. This is the mind desiring to revere salvation's science from out of the Bible to conquer their former personal and devotional self. Being *dead* with that spiritual understanding our faith, while internally *alive* to the knowledge of the living God's will and wisdom, now lives as being *dead* to the influence of the religious world. All that are literally dead cannot bring any imagination to their mind nor will their self to move, for "all go unto one place; all are of the dust, and all turn to dust again."[183] We, being philosophically *alive*, are *dead* to religious error in thought and in deed, that through the body of our belief we should honor the new code of being.[184]

12. By honoring the new mind of devotion regenerated through the living God's wisdom, we will never fail to honor the character of that wisdom and its experience. The war between the inward mind and the natural devotional mind is far from easy and cannot be done alone. Presumption must be given up in order to channel the power and the confidence of *creation's* wisdom.[185] The Bible does not therefore leave us ignorant about how our conversation, in order to receive showers of blessing, can do well.

14. We are counseled that the manners of the old devotional mind are to be separated from our conversation by self-denial so that its body of error may be found without an *inhabitant*. By resting in the character of the living God's present commandment for devotional wellbeing, our confidence may be found spotless and blameless through

---

182   Romans 6:6
183   Ecclesiastes 3:20
184   Ephesians 4:13
185   Isaiah 45:8

an active faith in the experience of that commandment. Our conversation should not practice any *thing* contrary to the experience within the living God's wisdom. Should our conversation's conscience remain under the *wings* of that wisdom to accept its showers of understanding, unhealthy personal and devotional habits and tendencies will vanish.

15. We become a problem to our self when we begin to personally put down our old religious constitution for uplifting the new. Through days and months and years we have accustomed ourselves to become numb to the Bible's *voice*, making it difficult to embrace an inward journey. Physical actions please the natural conversation, it loves the taste of theories, but the process of *holiness* calls for us to learn of our internal warfare to rest in intelligence greater than our own. This is why it says, "Take up thy bed, and walk."[186]

16. The *way* of continual blessing demands that our faith's intellect separate from our old devotional mind so that "all things are become new."[187] If the personal devotional body is in an unclean state of being, so too will be the natural mind. Grace must override philosophical complacency. The conversation cannot honor salvation's discipline while serving self. It is the responsibility of the conversation to search through the Bible's mind to support the newness of mind it would have. Doing so will lead to us edifying our faith's intellect.

17. The work of perfecting and reforming the conversation's conscience is for brining the mind of devotion closer to the living God's devotional character. Although the experience is inwardly trying, we do well to remember how it says, "He which soweth sparingly shall reap also sparingly; and he which soweth bountifully shall reap bountifully. Every man according as he purposeth in his heart, so let him give; not grudgingly, or of necessity: for God loveth a cheerful giver."[188]

18. "Let us draw near with a true heart in full assurance of faith, having our hearts sprinkled from an evil conscience, and our bodies washed with pure water,"[189] that we may live by an exercised faith

---

186   John 5:11
187   2 Corinthians 5:17
188   2 Corinthians 9:6,7
189   Hebrews 10:22

through the wisdom of the living God's *voice*. "Though the Lord give you the bread of adversity, and the water of affliction,"[190] "if thou continue in his goodness,"[191] "thine ears shall hear a word behind thee, saying, This is the way, walk ye in it, when ye turn to the right hand, and when ye turn to the left."[192]

---

190   Isaiah 30:20
191   Romans 11:22
192   Isaiah 30:21

7

Watch and Consider

1. It is written, "Consider your ways."[193] "Return ye now every one from his evil way, and make your ways and your doings good."[194]

2. "Ye have sown much, and bring in little; ye eat, but ye have not enough; ye drink, but ye are not filled with drink; ye clothe you, but there is none warm; and he that earneth wages earneth wages to put it into a bag with holes."[195] "Behold, thou art made whole: sin no more, lest a worse thing come unto thee."[196] "Blessed are those servants, whom the lord when he cometh shall find watching."[197]

3. Through a right heart in personal and devotional well doing, a sure testimony of our service to the living God's wisdom will show

---

193   Haggai 1:5
194   Jeremiah 18:11
195   Haggai 1:6
196   John 5:14
197   Luke 12:37

through our commitment to the sound of its *voice*. It is for our conversation, if we so choose, to dissect our heart by this wisdom, and to call a council over the irrational thoughts of our mind, to the end that thorough care may be given to the acknowledgment of wellbeing for learning what is healthy and practical. Our understanding is to confess, "Thou hast maintained my right and my cause."[198]

4. Our conversation must know that the Bible's wisdom is its guide.[199] Our conversation must know to let that counsel establish its thoughts and feelings.[200] This is why it says, "Fear the LORD, and serve him in truth with all your heart: for consider how great things he hath done for you,"[201] and, "Consider the wondrous works of God."[202]

5. A reviving character is added to our conversation and wonderfully maintained when doing right by the Bible's present wisdom, bringing the private lessons learned in its classroom into the life. Should we do this, it says, "Thou shalt have treasure in heaven: and come, take up the cross, and follow me."[203] Hereafter our faith, immersing its self in this learning experience, is to say, "Praise him, ye heavens of heavens, and ye waters that be above the heavens,"[204] and, "Thy truth reacheth unto the clouds."[205]

6. The *treasure* that will be ours if we will but sincerely honor the living God's wisdom is edifying showers of blessing. The treasure *above* is ours, but the only way for us to receive that refreshing is by abandoning our former train of devotional thought to make the culture of the living God's will our habit. The saying is then true: "Blessed be the God and Father of our Lord Jesus Christ, who hath blessed us with all spiritual blessings."[206]

---

198   Psalms 9:4
199   Hebrews 13:5,6
200   Proverbs 4:26; Proverbs 16:2
201   1 Samuel 12:24
202   Job 37:14
203   Mark 10:21
204   Psalms 148:4
205   Psalms 108:4
206   Ephesians 1:3

7. Our example is everything to our profession. Our work of love and faith when enduring salvation's trial against our former devotional mind will prove beneficial to another who may be weak in nature, or spiritually anxious. If the end of our profession is simply a reflection of self, we labor after a presumptuous hope. Note the mind to exemplify: "If I do not the works of my Father, believe me not. But if I do, though ye believe not me, believe the works: that ye may know, and believe, that the Father is in me, and I in him."[207]

8. Without an outward expression of the inward manifestation of the living God's wisdom upon the mind, there is no proof of our experience; we are as salt "neither fit for the land, nor yet for the dunghill."[208] If our conversation is not honoring the Bible's wisdom through its chief principle of government, we are serving self, our god is our *flesh*, and out of policy we prolong a false experience. This is why it says, "Know ye not, that to whom ye yield yourselves servants to obey, his servants ye are to whom ye obey; whether of sin unto death, or of obedience unto righteousness?"[209]

9. It is that putting on of "the new man, which is renewed in knowledge after the image of him that created him,"[210] that gives *life* to our experience, "for our rejoicing is this, the testimony of our conscience."[211] Our conversation is not to believe that it receives praise or favor for what it does; it says, "He respecteth not any that are wise of heart."[212] The living God knows the motive behind the conversation's intention; "all things are naked and opened unto the eyes of him with whom we have to do."[213]

10. Should our conversation, as is depicted by the character of the living God's wisdom, fail to properly lift up its standard of wellness, there is no way that it can remain consecrated to the living God, but rather it causes its own separation from *life's* course of learning.

---

207   John 10:37,38
208   Luke 14:35
209   Romans 6:16
210   Colossians 3:10
211   2 Corinthians 1:12
212   Job 37:24
213   Hebrews 4:13

Thus, after receiving necessary correction to our conversation, it is well to take advantage of that correction, learning of and exercising the wisdom acquired to keep our faith sincere.[214]

11. The Bible, knowing the religious deception our faith initially entertains, counsels our conversation to turn away from its former devotional confidence. Because if fantasy did alleviate the human being, then we who turn, and hear, and commit to do, are horribly sorry individuals. We are sorry individuals because we have, in vain, left what comforts our heart. Yet the Bible's wisdom is a living witness to the journey of our faith's growth and development.[215]

12. We who carry breath are alive for the reception of *mercy* to receive an outpouring of understanding that devotional regeneration may be given, even as it is written, "Ask ye the LORD rain in the time of the latter rain."[216] Our heart still beats, our insides and vitals still function, for the purpose of considering the habits we have taken to support our *life*, these habits being the means whereby we personally and devotionally *sleep*. This we are to do so that we may withdraw from ignorance, which is why it says, "Wash you, make you clean; put away the evil of your doing,"[217] and "Learn to do well."[218]

13. There is, along with no *sleep* or *death*, no *confusion* in the living God's philosophy. Our conversation will *live* if it will commit its self to know that wisdom's will. All that we have ever thought to keep us from the living God, all that we imagine to make it impossible to know our Creator, every doubt or fear settled into the heart from tradition, or our own self-cultivated superstition, is come to an end in the *arms* of this spiritual understanding. We don't have to look far for help when we turn away from our former religious confidence, nor do we have to guess at where we may learn *creation's* present government. By

---

214   Galatians 4:9
215   1 Corinthians 15:19,20
216   Zechariah 10:1
217   Isaiah 1:16
218   Isaiah 1:17
                    39

beholding it we "are changed into the same image from glory to glory, even as by the Spirit of the Lord."[219]

14. "The word of God is quick, and powerful, and sharper than any twoedged sword, piercing even to the dividing asunder of soul and spirit, and of the joints and marrow, and is a discerner of the thoughts and intents of the heart."[220] "The people of Nin'eveh believed God, and proclaimed a fast, and put on sackcloth, from the greatest of them even to the least of them,"[221] and because, by guilt, they accepted their conversation to be worthy of *death*, when repenting, "God saw their works, that they turned from their evil way; and God repented of the evil, that he had said that he would do unto them; and he did it not."[222]

15. Herein is our example. We should not become discouraged, or even turn to a contrary form of understanding when the living God's *voice* plainly shows us our need to refrain form religious error. We are expected to turn away; intellectual and spiritual *death* is not a condition supported by the living God. Because we turn aside to consider what is going on with us, it is understood that, because we are mindful of the intention behind the living God's wisdom, we want a restored mind of service. Because we lack understanding, and even truly reasonable affection, it doesn't mean that we fail to consider how we manage self and endorse ignorance. This is why it says, "Make you a new heart and a new spirit: for why will ye die"?[223]

16. The living God will not, without our consent, change our heart. By cooperating with the living God's counsel for devotional betterment, that counsel can and will, and most emphatically, make our heart new. This is why it says, "I will restore health unto thee, and I will heal thee of thy wounds."[224]

17. There is not a natural desire within our human being for right wellbeing. Should one seek, of their own will, to change their heart,

---

219   2 Corinthians 3:18
220   Hebrews 4:12
221   Jonah 3:5
222   Jonah 3:10
223   Ezekiel 18:31
224   Jeremiah 30:17

they will either crumble from heartache or quit the reformation. Yet of that wisdom declaring, "I create new,"[225] and of that wisdom who is "the everlasting God, the LORD, the Creator,"[226] your conversation is not indebted to "be not conformed to this world,"[227] but rather to be "transformed by the renewing of your mind, that ye may prove what is that good, and acceptable, and perfect, will of God."[228] By this wisdom's perfecting grace, *he* is truly "the creator of Israel."[229]

18. There is a different experience expected for us from the one we are familiar with. Without the living God's wisdom convicting the heart of its wrong against both self and that wisdom, the steps taken for a reform are done in vain; we neither know why we are following these things nor for what benefit they serve when we are stimulated by *meat* within the heart. "But they that wait upon the LORD shall renew their strength,"[230] therefore to say that we expect living God to change our heart is to attribute a quality to *God* that is not there, and to completely undermine, and show a lack of an understanding in the power and wisdom of the Bible's ministry of healing.

19. Let it be said, should we demand a change of heart from *above*, "Ye do err, not knowing the scriptures, nor the power of God."[231] "Have ye not read that which was spoken unto you by God, saying, I am the God of Abraham, and the God of Isaac, and the God of Jacob? God is not the God of the dead, but of the living."[232] "God is a Spirit: and they that worship him must worship him in spirit and in truth,"[233] "for if ye live after the flesh, ye shall die: but if ye through the Spirit do mortify the deeds of the body, ye shall live. For as many as are led by the Spirit of God, they are the sons of God."[234]

---

225   Isaiah 65:17
226   Isaiah 40:28
227   Romans 12:2
228   Romans 12:2
229   Isaiah 43:15
230   Isaiah 40:31
231   Matthew 22:29
232   Matthew 22:31,32
233   John 4:24
234   Romans 8:13,14

20. Should we correctly honor the Bible's counsel, our conversation will declare, *"Cleanse me* from my sin."[235] It will pray, *"Create in me* a clean heart, O God; *and renew* a right spirit within me,"[236] and, *"Restore* unto me the joy of thy salvation; and *uphold me* with thy free spirit."[237] This is why it says, "I am the LORD, your Holy One, *the creator* of Israel, your King."[238]

21. The Bible's wisdom desires our conversation to renew its mind so that it would learn of its new heart. By cooperating with its course's requirements, meeting and lifting up every one of its standards within our sphere, we are to receive promised showers of blessing to advance our conversation in its intended *nature*, and with a menu able to edify other minds.

22. The Bible cannot mysteriously make our hearts pleasing to its wisdom without our consent, and will not do so by force. The conversation must mentally and inwardly comply with its wisdom's manner of devotion because grace alone is not enough for creation. This is why it says, "Unto him that is able to do exceeding abundantly above all that we ask or think, according to the power that worketh in us,"[239] and, "Examine yourselves, whether ye be in the faith; prove your own selves."[240]

---

235   Psalm 51:2
236   Psalm 51:10
237   Psalm 51:12
238   Isaiah 43:15
239   Ephesians 3:20
240   2 Corinthians 13:5

8

His Mind in Us

1. *Hope* and *mercy* are at the living God's right hand. This *hope* and *mercy* is a doctrine of devotional redemption. The wisdom therefore stating, "I am he that liveth, and was dead; and behold, I am alive for evermore,"[241] is that wisdom perfecting the aroma of our supplications. This is why it says, "Whatsoever ye shall ask in my name, that will I do, that the Father may be glorified in the Son."

2. Our hope and our joy, our peace and our understanding, is that wisdom living for our devotional development. Its joy is made full when its devotional character can rest within our faith's confidence. This wisdom is happy when our conversation repents and moves on from past religious error, adding to its mind an edifying spirit for developing fruit similar to its character. This wisdom's takes joy in living as our

---

241   Revelation 1:18

faith's intercessor, as it says, "Striving according to his working, which worketh in me mightily."[242]

3. From understanding the hope and pleasure of being called the living God's creation, our conversation is made free to carry a joy within that will allow us to become unmoved at trials set before us. From faithfully understanding how the living God loves, every effort to conform to the character of the Bible's wisdom will be right and sincere. Through the joy of the hope of its manner of salvation, our conversation is to personally continue "endeavoring to keep the unity of the Spirit in the bond of peace."[243]

4. There is no *sadness* in the living God's "joy," nor is their *grief*. Though we, for a right understanding, suffer inward anguish,[244] we enjoy such a challenge that we may reach closer to knowing how to properly manage our conversation, even like as it says, "What things were gain to me, those I counted loss for Christ."[245] The journey is not easy,"[246] which is why one must never forget that "in all these things we are more than conquerors through him that loved us."[247]

5. Because the living God's "mercy is great above the heavens,"[248] and this "truth reacheth unto the clouds,"[249] our conversation has a very great hope. The beginning of this hope is according to the saying, "I will pour out my spirit unto you,"[250] so that it may be said, "I will make known my words unto you."[251] The influence of the Bible's wisdom is entered into our heart so that our conversation may be created.[252]

6. This wonderful hope is the joy of the conversation valuing creation's grace, daily developing and maintaining, while exercising control over the mind within their *body* through that wisdom, a respect

---

242   Colossians 1:29
243   Ephesians 4:3
244   2 Corinthians 5:2
245   Philippians 3:7
246   Philippians 3:13,14
247   Romans 8:37
248   Psalms 108:4
249   Psalms 108:4
250   Proverbs 1:23
251   Proverbs 1:23
252   Colossians 3:10

for their faith's higher learning. Our conversation's conscience will be made perfect as it accepts that wisdom within it. By looking unto the example of the living God's chief messenger, our efforts and our intention will be justified.[253]

7. Our conversation is miserable and does not quite know it. It is wretched, yet, because of our unsettled natural condition, it is personally ignored. Our conversation is poor, and blind, and naked, refusing to place its self into the *dust* for the reviving and reforming of its conscience.

8. But our conversation will be made joyful when willingly accepting that it fails to exists without the living God's promise and remedy. It is the joy of knowing that its condition is to be redeemed that we willingly live our life for that commandment, its honor, its favor, and its blessing. Hereafter we come to learn the saying, "O Lord, by these things men live, and in all these things is the life of my spirit."[254]

9. No one can take away the joy the Bible's wisdom commits to our conversation's mind. It does not will for our conversation's conscience to pass away, but would have every conversation dawning the likeness of its devotional character. Therefore "meditate upon these things; give thyself wholly to them; that thy profiting may appear to all. Take heed unto thyself, and unto the doctrine; continue in them: for in doing this thou shalt both save thyself, and them that hear thee."[255]

10. The living God's wisdom is given to reveal our devotional error to our conscience. A form of mourning for our faith's condition is to commence when inwardly impressed by this wisdom, the point being that "we might be justified by faith."[256] Because even the Bible admits our natural religious conversation to be sinful,[257] our conversation is to learn of and adopt the Bible's present course of learning.[258] We must know that our confidence in our experience occurs as we exercise faith

253   Job 11:15,16
254   Isaiah 38:16
255   1 Timothy 4:15,16
256   Galatians 3:24
257   Galatians 3:22
258   Hebrews 3:14

on the Bible's present philosophy. Through a patient and continual effort in well doing, we may reflect the *image* contained within the scriptures, which is why it says, "Understanding is a wellspring of life unto him that hath it."[259]

11. Only the understanding given to us by a living experience can prepare our heart to grow in grace with the living God's spiritual understanding. True joy is seen through the Bible's complete doctrine, allowing the careful observer to learn of the privilege of experiencing inward and devotional wellbeing. As we search for better understanding the Bible's philosophy, its wisdom will be given to us so that we may comprehend the depth of *creation's* science for our human and devotional condition.

12. The joy of the living God's kindness within the conversation's conscience settles in the heart and mind and impregnates the entire devotional life with peace, love, hope, patience, and temperance. "We through the Spirit wait for the hope of righteousness by faith,"[260] which hope is our faith's joy, and that joy being the liberty of our conversation to commit its entire being "to him that judgeth righteously."[261]

13. That hope purifies the thoughts and feelings of the reforming belief. The conversation joying in the living God's manner of love, waiting for "the acknowledging of the truth which is after godliness,"[262] sets to its self the same faith as the living God's chief apostle to receive the end of that faith, even a heart "unblameable in holiness"[263] causing us "to increase and abound in love one toward another, and toward all men."[264]

14. The hope of possessing the intended devotional character should be our comfort in every trial. Through quietly relinquishing the heart to the will of the Bible's wisdom, the conversation of the living God's chief minister was made perfect by what it suffered,[265] and to us

---

259 Proverbs 16:22
260 Galatians 5:5
261 1 Peter 2:23
262 Titus 1:1
263 1 Thessalonians 3:13
264 1 Thessalonians 3:12
265 Hebrews 5:8

this same promise is given. Whatever befalls us, whatever is confusing or perplexing, whatever will send us into a rage or even into disappointment, these things are given so that our conversation may "be strengthened with might by his Spirit in the inner man; that Christ may dwell in your hearts by faith."[266]

15. Just as the living God's chief minister lived every moment through the strength of the Bible's wisdom, so too our conversation is to do the same. It is the knowledge of this hope; which wisdom is derived from having the conversation perfectly created through philosophical grief, pain, and trial; that brings devotional comfort that cannot be disturbed. It is through this work of dedicating the conversation to the living God's wisdom that we come "to know the love of Christ, which passeth knowledge."[267]

---

266   Ephesians 3:16,17
267   Ephesians 3:19

9

A Living Experience

1. There is a need to cultivate a living experience not only in the living God's wisdom, but also in the self-reflection that is attached to it. "The doctrine which is according to godliness,"[268] or "the acknowledging of the truth which is after godliness,"[269] is our faith's main educational source to never have it said of us, "Never able to come to the knowledge of the truth."[270] Such learning, seeing as how "the excellency of knowledge is, that wisdom giveth life to them that have it,"[271] is "the knowledge of wisdom."[272] This "life" is our only means for developing a right devotional character.[273]

---

268   1 Timothy 6:3
269   Titus 1:1
270   2 Timothy 3:7
271   Ecclesiastes 7:12
272   Proverbs 24:14
273   Philippians 3:9

2. "That I may know him,"[274] should be written on our heart by our own persevering efforts to learn of and prove the Bible's philosophy. The point of this experience is for our conversation to possess "all things that pertain unto life and godliness, through the knowledge of him that hath called us to glory and virtue,"[275] and "according as his divine power hath given unto us."[276]

3. As the Bible's wisdom convicts our conversation's conscience, we are to look self in the face, courageously rejecting the feeling of being uncomfortable. When "the desire of all nations shall come"[277] to our heart to arrest our thoughts and feelings, convincing us of "the love that God hath to us,"[278] we do well to not fight its manner of discipline. Our conversation is to exercise faith in the wisdom empowering the living God's will that we may have "the victory that overcometh the world."[279]

4. The knowledge gained from exercising faith on the living God's words is to re-educate our faith's mind and appetite into a manner of wellness that "cannot be gotten for gold, neither shall silver be weighed for the price thereof. It cannot be valued with the gold of O'phir, with the precious onyx, or the sapphire."[280] "No mention shall be made of coral, or of pearls: for the price of wisdom is above rubies."[281] Personal devotional wisdom is the prize,[282] yet it is rejected,[283] and for doing so, "My people are destroyed,"[284] it is written.

5. It is the Bible's intention to make sure that our conversation is "full of goodness, filled with knowledge, able also to admonish one

---

274   Philippians 3:10
275   2 Peter 1:3
276   2 Peter 1:3
277   Haggai 2:7
278   1 John 4:16
279   1 John 5:4
280   Job 28:15,16
281   Job 28:18
282   Proverbs 20:15
283   Hosea 8:3
284   Hosea 4:6

another."[285] So that it may increase in understanding,[286] our conversation is to exercise the wisdom put within it. By placing into the *life* the lessons learned in the classroom of salvation's science, our conversation is to grow in knowledge of its purpose, to the end godly affection may be the fragrance of our speech and gestures.

6. According to the Bible, that we may "obtain gladness and joy"[287] from abiding by the counsel, "Acquaint now thyself with him,"[288] our conversation is to possess a mind "of sorrows, and acquainted with grief."[289] This is the only experience from which "my people shall know my name," says this wisdom. Self needs to be continually sacrificed to the living God's wisdom in order for us to receive the promised newness in thought and in feeling, which is why it says, "If any man will come after me, let him deny himself, and take up his cross daily, and follow me."[290]

7. Yet how is it fulfilled, and even at this time, "The children which thou shalt have, after thou hast lost the other, shall say again in thine ears, The place is too strait for me: give place to me that I may dwell"?[291]

8. At this time, the living God calls conversations that will be called to "sanctification of the Spirit and belief of the truth."[292] This is why it says, "Look unto Abraham your father, and unto Sarah that bare you."[293] We are called to learn from *he* who "staggered not at the promise of God through unbelief,"[294] and to mark our paths as *she* who "judged him faithful who had promised."[295] "Being fully persuaded that, what he had promised, he was able also to perform,"[296] Abraham

---

285   Romans 15:14
286   Philippians 1:9
287   Isaiah 51:11
288   Job 22:21
289   Isaiah 53:3
290   Luke 9:23
291   Isaiah 49:20
292   2 Thessalonians 2:13
293   Isaiah 51:2
294   Romans 4:20
295   Hebrews 11:11
296   Romans 4:21

"against hope believed in hope,"[297] "and therefore it was imputed to him for righteousness."[298]

9. Our conversation is to trust the creative power of their devotional experience.[299] The conversation of the living God's chief apostle "took upon him the form of a servant, and was made in the likeness of men,"[300] that by its example of self-sacrifice we would, in hope of the resurrection of our devotional mind, put our former spiritual understanding in a perpetual prison. This refreshed conversation, to the end we may "be kindly affectioned one to another with brotherly love,"[301] will reflect the intended devotional mind, which is a conversation concerned only with the will of the living God's wisdom.[302]

10. Before we can love like the living God, our conversation must "be filled with the knowledge of his will in all wisdom and spiritual understanding."[303] This is why it says, "By his knowledge shall my righteous servant justify many."[304]

11. The knowledge of the Bible's wisdom advises its student to state: "I count all things but loss...that I may know him, and the power of his resurrection, and the fellowship of his sufferings, being made conformable unto his death."[305] Only by consenting to experiencing practical godliness by a living experience with the Bible's wisdom can we become one body "knit together in love, and unto all riches of the full assurance of understanding."[306]

12. Experiencing inward turmoil from the Bible's philosophy, the living God's chief apostle gained the knowledge, or the experience, necessary to discover and demonstrate the doctrine of justification.

---

297   Romans 4:18
298   Romans 4:22
299   Romans 4:24; Romans 6:5
300   Philippians 2:7
301   Romans 12:10
302   1 Peter 4:2
303   Colossians 1:9
304   Isaiah 53:11
305   Philippians 3:8-10
306   Colossians 2:2

Herein is our example, because "though he were yet a Son, yet learned he obedience by the things which he suffered."[307]

13. This Rabbi's suffering is a form of learning our faith's re-education needs to adopt. Until our conversation can first surrender its self to the will of the living God's wisdom, we will never come to know the point of a living experience or the purpose of true education. A negligent and stubborn heart is proof that the conversation does not care to know the living God both personally and devotionally.

14. Afflicting the soul with the Bible's words, and through reflecting on self by those words, is the only means whereby our heart will awaken to its need; this is why it says, "Awake to righteousness, and sin not; for some have not the knowledge of God."[308] This knowledge is the wisdom of a living experience whereby "I die daily"[309] according to that wisdom's will. This should be the theme of devotional education from morning until the evening.

15. There needs to be more of a consistent effort to not only search or examine the Bible, but to allow what is found to be brought into the heart. There is a reason why it says, "The fear of the LORD tendeth to life."[310]

16. There needs to be more of a consistent effort to learn of and do the Bible's approach to practical godliness. Only by a living and personal experience in and with the Bible's philosophy may the conversation be transformed.

17. Our faith's intellect is to be renewed by knowledge concerning the living God's devotional character. Our conversation is to mimic the Bible's right mind, meaning, if we would suffer our conversation to draw "nigh unto death, not regarding his life,"[311] our faith would learn of and adopt the intended manner of devotion, confessing, "I will very

---

307   Hebrews 5:8,9
308   1 Corinthians 15:34
309   1 Corinthians 15:31
310   Proverbs 19:23
311   Philippians 2:30

gladly spend and be spent for you; though the more abundantly I love you, the less I be loved."[312]

18. Self-sacrificing love is the foundation of the Bible's wisdom. The purpose of re-educating the conversation's thoughts and feelings not only through a process scriptural understanding, but also through character development by living what has become understood, is to have the effect of creation's science sealed within our inward person. Hereafter our conversation will "shew out of a good conversation his works with meekness of wisdom."[313]

---

312   2 Corinthians 12:15
313   James 3:13

10

Add to Faith
the Knowledge of Wisdom

1. It is written, "The LORD giveth wisdom: out of his mouth cometh knowledge and understanding."[314] In another place it is written, "Man doth not live by bread alone, but by every word that proceedeth out of the mouth of the LORD doth man live."[315]

2. Knowledge and understanding comes from out of the living God's *mouth*, and if we would apply our hearts to that *voice*, the result will be inward and devotional health. From actively depending on what comes out of the Bible's mind, we can have "the spirit of wisdom and revelation in the knowledge of him,"[316] seeing as how "by his knowledge the

---

314   Proverbs 2:6
315   Deuteronomy 8:2,3
316   Ephesians 1:17

depths are broken up, and the clouds drop down the dew."[317] By doing that knowledge, the ground of our heart will undergo a process of being broken up, even like as it says, "Break up your fallow ground,"[318] or, "Take away the foreskin of your heart."[319]

3. "Let thine heart retain my words,"[320] it says, "keep them in the midst of thine heart."[321] "Receive my words, and hide my commandments,"[322] "incline thine ear,"[323] "apply thine heart,"[324] "write them upon the table of thine heart."[325] "Bind them continually upon thine heart,"[326] we are counseled. "Keep my commandments, and live; and my law as the apple of thine eye."[327] "Then shalt thou walk in thy way safely, and thy foot shall not stumble."[328]

4. There is a personal work that the conversation must do if it would know the promise, "He shall come unto us as the rain, as the latter and former rain unto the earth."[329] If we would have our conversation's conscience refreshed, we must remain in active communion with the living God's words "until the day dawn, and the day star arise in your hearts."[330]

5. It is not safe to believe that the living God will transform our heart without any effort on our part. This is why we are initially counseled, before that transformation may take place, "Giving all diligence, add."[331] "Circumcise therefore the foreskin of your heart, and be no more stiffnecked,"[332] it is written, and, "Thoroughly amend your ways

---

317   Proverbs 3:20
318   Jeremiah 4:4
319   Jeremiah 4:4
320   Proverbs 4:4
321   Proverbs 4:21
322   Proverbs 2:1
323   Proverbs 2:2
324   Proverbs 2:2
325   Proverbs 3:3
326   Proverbs 6:21
327   Proverbs 7:2
328   Proverbs 3:23
329   Hosea 6:3
330   2 Peter 1:19
331   2 Peter 1:5
332   Deuteronomy 10:16

and your doings,"[333] says the prophet, because the knowledge of the living God's wisdom is gained from learning of and applying to the Bible's words, even as it says, "Learn to do well."[334]

6. The prize gained to creation's assembly from sincerely honoring the Bible's words is[335] "sweet to the soul, and health to the bones."[336] It is for us to get, possess, gain, and exercise the practice of the living God's "sweet health," which "sweet health" is the kindness attributed to the conversation's conscience through the living God's wisdom. It is the conversation's responsibility to chase the spirit of wisdom by the spirit of self-sacrifice through the spirit of faith, even as it is written, "Get wisdom, get understanding,"[337] and, "Get wisdom: and with all thy getting get understanding."[338]

7. The living God's knowledge is given when experiencing its counsel, to the end our conversation may confess, "By these things men live, and in all these things is the life of my spirit."[339] Surely, then, "if thou criest after knowledge"[340] and "liftest up thy voice for understanding,"[341] "if thou seekest her"[342] and "searchest for her as for hid treasures,"[343] "then shalt thou understand the fear of the LORD, and find the knowledge of God."[344]

8. The living God's wisdom is the knowledge and understanding of the Bible's intention and science, and this knowledge of wisdom comes by enduring the re-education of our faith's intellect. From honoring that wisdom acquired through that re-education, experience is added unto us, but what is the report? It says, "They hearkened not, nor inclined their ear, but walked in the counsels and in the imagination of

---

333   Jeremiah 7:5
334   Isaiah 1:17
335   2 Peter 1:1
336   Proverbs 16:24
337   Proverbs 4:5
338   Proverbs 4:7
339   Isaiah 38:16
340   Proverbs 2:3
341   Proverbs 2:3
342   Proverbs 2:4
343   Proverbs 2:4
344   Proverbs 2:5

their evil heart, and went backward, and not forward."[345] It may not be so easy to learn of and apply to the Bible's words, and we may experience difficulty in understanding its advice, but should we endure, well-being awaits us.[346]

9. The knowledge spoken of in the Bible is not a knowledge that is gained by familiarity with religious rumors or theories. This knowledge cannot be handled as a *body* of *truths* or *facts* accumulated over the course of time and handwritten by theologians. The living God's knowledge is, due to living the Bible's words, practical wisdom gained by suffering the conversation to know humiliation, pain, agony, and grief. So "consider in thine heart, that, as a man chasteneth his son, so the LORD thy God chasteneth thee."[347] The humble and disciplined conversation will receive its revelation to make its experience real.[348]

10. By feeling their human experience, the individual will be brought to search the scriptures for a remedy, enlightening their mind from diligently searching for the Bible's opinion on the matter. The conversation, according to the Bible's wisdom, must have discretion, or must exercise, for understanding its words, power over the will to refrain from being slaves to devotional appetite and passion, or slaves to "the imagination of the thoughts of the heart."[349]

11. The Bible's wisdom is for devotional soundness, as it is written, "A sound heart is the life of the flesh."[350] This is why it says, "When wisdom entereth into thine heart, and knowledge is pleasant unto thy soul; discretion shall preserve thee, understanding shall keep thee."[351]

12. The spirit of our mind is to endure the trial of its faith with the hope that it will be refreshed from the experience. If we allow the Bible to teach, if we allow our self to embrace its counsel, we will come to not only know our issues and their remedy, but in faithfulness "thou shalt

---

345   Jeremiah 7:24
346   Hebrews 12:11
347   Deuteronomy 8:5
348   Deuteronomy 8:2
349   1 Chronicles 29:18
350   Proverbs 14:30
351   Proverbs 2:10,11

know the LORD."[352] From the knowledge that is given, our conversation will be kept and preserved from contrary religious manners because we've submitted to creation's science by faith. We've cried and howled for help and trusted in the Bible's words to heal, therefore being delivered from inward trouble, it is that "our lips may keep knowledge."[353]

13. Our conversation's betterment is through the soundness of its heart. Wisdom is counsel, and our experience with the living God's words will deliver us wise counsel that we may keep our mind safe. Our "teaching and admonishing one another in psalms and hymns and spiritual songs";[354] which *songs* are of our faithful experience; is to be of a wisdom causing us to be "as a dew from the LORD."[355] It is the Bible's intention that our conversation's conscience experience regeneration in thought and in feeling.

14. Wisdom is counsel, and counsel is given to the prudent, or to the one maintaining a diligent investigation. If wisdom is wise counsel given to the one desiring to maintain a true devotional education, then truly the living God's science becomes "the power of God, and the wisdom of God."[356] A mind set to respond to the call, "Take my yoke upon you, and learn of me,"[357] is a *life* set to claim true wisdom by actively picking up and exercising the Bible's words. One "of understanding shall attain to wise counsels"[358] through a meaningful experience, and the understanding gained turns into wisdom when the experience becomes real.

15. "The wisdom of the prudent is to understand his way."[359] Right knowledge is acquired only from living through something by faith. Should we honor the *ladder* that *Peter* counsels us to consider, we will "neither be barren nor unfruitful in the knowledge of our Lord."[360]

---

352   Hosea 2:20
353   Proverbs 5:2
354   Colossians 3:16
355   Micah 5:7
356   1 Corinthians 1:24
357   Matthew 11:29
358   Proverbs 1:5
359   Proverbs 14:8
360   2 Peter 1:8

"The excellency of knowledge is, that wisdom giveth life,"[361] therefore "happy is the man that findeth wisdom,"[362] seeing as how "she is a tree of life to them that lay hold upon her."[363]

16. "A prudent man concealeth knowledge"[364] that he "may have right to the tree of life,"[365] and in return is "crowned with knowledge."[366] Only by burying what is learned within the heart can the heart reveal what is inside of it; this is why it says, "For as he thinketh in his heart, so is he."[367] Only by laying our heart to *rest* may we then have this testimony: "Thy word have I hid in mine heart, that I might not sin against thee."[368]

17. The Bible's wisdom cannot be gained without mental and inward activity. The Bible's love cannot reach the soul in doubt or in stubbornness. The experience gained "addeth learning"[369] because the will has been convinced to surrender at the sight of a healing doctrine. When once the thoughts are given over to meditate on the illustration of the living God's chief apostle suffering the tree, the heart will declare, "We hid as it were our faces from him."[370]

18. The scriptures took its wisdom and "made him to be sin for us, who knew no sin: that we might be made the righteousness of God in him."[371] The prize for experiencing our conversation in greater philosophical health cannot be paid without a willing and a living sacrifice. To do anything for the sake of the living God's wisdom is to do all things by its spirit of unselfish love for the living God's will.

19. By honoring the commandments of the Bible's present science, by reverencing every word of wisdom and knowledge from its spiritual understanding, learning is added to the mind and faith, love, and life to

---

361   Ecclesiastes 7:12
362   Proverbs 3:13
363   Proverbs 3:18
364   Proverbs 12:23
365   Revelation 22:14
366   Proverbs 14:18
367   Proverbs 23:7
368   Psalms 119:11
369   Proverbs 16:23
370   Isaiah 53:3
371   2 Corinthians 5:21

the heart. This is why it says, "They also that erred in spirit shall come to understanding, and they that murmured shall learn doctrine."[372] The living God's love placed into the soul from temperately searching the scriptures to acquire knowledge of self is the only way to conceive an acceptable devotional character; it is the only way of ensuring our faith's conscience does not work against us.

20. The living God's doctrine is to carry us through our living experience, this is why it is written, "He shall drink of the brook in the way: therefore shall he lift up the head."[373] The living God's chief minister drank from "the rivers, the floods, the brooks of honey and butter,"[374] therefore it is written of him, "Butter and honey shall he eat, that he may know to refuse the evil, and choose the good."[375] It was this Rabbi who, just like us, learned how to exercise his faith in the living God's benevolence, who also benefited from that exercise when inwardly disturbed.[376]

21. "Surely the churning of milk bringeth forth butter,"[377] and as honey is good, "so shall the knowledge of wisdom be unto thy soul,"[378] seeing as how the good things of the living God's mind are to be given "by reason of use."[379] We ought to then know that "bodily exercise profiteth little: but godliness is profitable unto all things."[380]

22. Progress in the intended devotional experience occurs only through positively agitating the conversation's conscience. Distress of mind will cause the heart to search, pray, and reflect in agony by faith. The living God's chief minister has proven that there is no other way to overcome an unstable devotional mind than to subdue its imaginations through the Bible's wisdom. The suffering of his devotional mind made his conversation perfect, for he learned and gained new knowledge

---

372   Isaiah 29:24
373   Psalms 110:7
374   Job 20:17
375   Isaiah 7:15
376   Hebrews 5:7-9
377   Proverbs 30:33
378   Proverbs 24:14
379   Hebrews 5:14
380   1 Timothy 4:8

of personal and religious error, moving him to plead for strength to receive an understanding that he knew was not within his self.

23. Should we add this man's experience to our faith's training, we will add learning and understanding to our *tongue*, arriving at knowledge to live by. There is a lacking of *fruit* to conversations because it has not had its gifts multiplied. There is a lacking of the multiplying of *fruit* because it has yet to diligently add to its faith by self-regulation. "Phygel'lus and Hermog'enes"[381] are the *names* of conversations believing that the *hand* of *God* will magically appear to make them *perfect*.

24. "He that trusteth in his own heart is a fool"[382] and fails to remember how it says, "Guide thine heart in the way."[383] We are, that our conversation may "arise from the dead"[384] for "understanding what the will of the Lord is,"[385] to guide our own hearts to "awake to righteousness, and sin not."[386] We are to guide our thoughts to patiently wait for an understanding on what the Bible is saying, and are to guide our minds to remain diligent, faithful, and trusting in that experience to deliver its mental refreshing.[387]

25. "The sweetness of the lips increaseth learning,"[388] and the conversation diligently adding knowledge to their experience will gain the heart of the Bible through the heart of the Bible. This, for our faith's developing condition, is important. The living God's thoughts must be kept before our conversation's conscience or else the disposition to maintain wholesome *fruit* will grow sour.

26. The knowledge of the devotional victory gained by the living God's chief apostle must remain connected to the conversation or else the intention of the Bible's philosophy will be forgotten. The experience can only be valuable as the conversation endures the process of

---

381   2 Timothy 1:15
382   Proverbs 28:26
383   Proverbs 23:19
384   Ephesians 5:14
385   Ephesians 5:17
386   1 Corinthians 1:34
387   Zechariah 6:15
388   Proverbs 16:21

that philosophy and its science combining to perfectly edify the person. If there is no desire to sacrifice all that the conversation assumes to know, if the mind will not settle on the unfortunate sight of its condition for its recovery, its spirit will fade, its heart will grow numb to the Bible's invitation.

27. "Happy is the man whom God correcteth: therefore despise not the chastening of the Almighty: for he maketh sore, and bindeth up: he woundeth, and his hands make whole. He shall deliver thee in six troubles: yea, in seven there shall no evil touch thee."[389]

28. "For thou shalt be in league with the stones of the field: and the beasts of the field shall be at peace with thee. And thou shalt know that thy tabernacle shall be in peace; and thou shalt visit thy habitation, and shalt not sin."[390] "If thou prepare thine heart...then shalt thou lift up thy face without spot; yea, thou shalt be stedfast, and shalt not fear...Thou shalt be secure, because there is hope; yea, thou shalt dig about thee, and shalt take thy rest in safety."[391]

---

389   Job 5:17-19
390   Job 5:23,24
391   Job 11:13-18

11

Learning's Age

1. There is no greater time for our faith's mind to experience creation's present benevolence than when our faith is young, and this affirmed by how it says, "When Israel was a child, then I loved him."[392]

2. When young in the years of our faith, "the kindness and love of God our Saviour toward man"[393] is better accepted into the conscience, allowing us to more confidently say, "I applied mine heart to know, and to search, and to seek out wisdom, and the reason of things."[394] Like as a child, having no mind for what came before them and what should come after, so also when faith is developing, it is well to move the mind to freely consider all *things* within the Bible, for the heart has not yet established a perception of principles or theories to halt its

---

392   Hosea 11:1
393   Titus 3:4
394   Ecclesiastes 7:25

examination of its *voice*, and the conversation is not set by reason of old spiritual age.

3. From the moment our heart discerns within it a peculiar fondness for the living God's will, it is well for us to drop every belief within self to simply hear and do the counsel, "Seek ye out of the book of the LORD, and read."[395] There is no thing within self or within the religious world that can suffice for our faith's personal growth, which is why we are to "be dead with Christ from the rudiments of the world,"[396] and why, "if ye through the Spirit do mortify the deeds of the body, ye shall live."[397] An experimental faith is to add sober understanding to our faith's affection, and while such understanding is harder to come by when faith's years are old, all learning is easily accepted and done when our faith is young.

4. What separates the child from the adult is that while the adult perceives a set map of knowledge for a routine to grow comfortable with, the child, having no set map, is curious about all things for developing a map of understanding. This continuously evolving map is perpetually challenged by the child, providing them the opportunity to gather information together for shaping the way they view and interact with their world; this is why it says, "Except ye be converted, and become as little children, ye shall not enter into the kingdom of heaven."[398]

5. The goal is to own the religious character within the Bible's spiritual understanding, not the tradition of the religious world or some *religious* character from self's interpretation of that *world*. The Bible's philosophy is not the religious world's doctrine. Self, due to having no conscious disposition within it, cannot, in and of itself, discern whether or not that doctrine within the religious world is positive or negative. Self, being innately regulated by a natural mind, can never sincerely admit, "I know that in me (that is, in my flesh,) dwelleth no good thing."[399]

---

395   Isaiah 34:16
396   Colossians 2:20
397   Romans 8:13
398   Matthew 18:3
399   Romans 7:18

6. Having no good thing in my *flesh*, my understanding on temporal and *eternal things* is naturally backwards, and if I should remain in this condition while hopeful to experience the living God's goodness, my faith will grow old and harden under a routine, my mind no longer being free to exercise itself on the Bible's *voice* to procure knowledge for my conversation's wellbeing. Our faith's spiritual map closes when age is added to it, wherefore it is best, early on, to examine and do the commandment advancing the living God's will. This is why it says, "He that doeth the will of God abideth for ever."[400]

7. The eyes of our faith are never to grow dull. Should our faith ever enter into old age, seeing as how "we have received a commandment from the Father,"[401] it is a sign of negligence towards *creation's* present commandment. If we honor this commandment, our faith's years will never experience any thing contrary to a fresh and lively vigor, which is why it says, "Forget not my law; but let thine heart keep my commandments: for length of days, and long life, and peace, shall they add to thee."[402]

8. Here is a promise specifically designed for our faith's higher learning. "Everlasting life" for our faith and mind is the end of the living God's commandment, but without this "life," our faith and its intellect will suffer decay, which is why it is necessary to know and to experience the living God's present wisdom. "he that believeth on the Son hath everlasting life: and he that believeth not the Son shall not see life; but the wrath of God abideth on him."[403]

9. Seeing as how "the spirit giveth life,"[404] and seeing as how "a spirit hath not flesh and bones,"[405] we cannot expect a tangible or sensual belief on "God's" "Son" to suffice for the promised "life." To "believe on" is to hear and act out; as it says, "He that heareth my word, and believeth on him that sent me";[406] and if we are to hear and do

---

400 1 John 2:17
401 2 John 1:4
402 Proverbs 3:1,2
403 John 3:36
404 2 Corinthians 3:6
405 Luke 24:39
406 John 5:24

"the Son," then it is evident we are to accomplish the law of a spiritual course.

10. Now, because "wisdom giveth life to them that have it,"[407] we must understand "the Son" is a body of wisdom casting forth a life-current to the doer of it, which is why it says, "Let the word of Christ dwell in you richly in all wisdom."[408] The everlasting life promised by "the Son" is an everlasting flow of wisdom given by "the knowledge of the Son of God,"[409] which knowledge is "the law of the Spirit of life."[410] Our faith is to experience this law's higher inward learning, for when the living God's chief minister fulfilled the will of this commandment, he said, "I know that his commandment is life everlasting."[411]

11. This commandment is the Bible's wisdom for the maturation of our faith's mind so that we "might be filled with the knowledge of his will in all wisdom and spiritual understanding"[412] for "charity out of a pure heart, and of a good conscience, and of faith unfeigned."[413] Our faith and spirit need the "life" forwarded by this judgment, wherefore it is well for us to personally investigate and do this law when our faith is fresh. Years of avoiding faith's cultivation will halt the organs of our faith's *body* from properly developing and functioning.

12. Our faith has members that connect to the organs of our mind, and these bodies shoot charges back and forth as we prove the Bible's sayings: their marriage is the means whereby our heart may connect to our mind for the reception of the Bible's wisdom. The spirit of our mind retains understanding only as it personally discerns *creation's* commandment. Through this commandment the conversation's heart has material to prove for encouraging faith's developing hope on the living God's will and science.

13. Our faith must receive every opportunity to form a solid *body* for the good of our personal and devotional understanding. If it should

---

407   Ecclesiastes 7:12
408   Colossians 3:16
409   Ephesians 4:13
410   Romans 8:2
411   John 12:50
412   Colossians 1:9
413   1 Timothy 1:5

lack training, it will devastate the entire structure of our being, which compromises self's relation not only to its inward person, but also to the outside world. The cultivation of our young faith is the discipline we need in order to accept the counsel: "Know that ye were not redeemed with corruptible things, as silver and gold, from your vain conversation received by tradition from your fathers."[414]

14. Personal faith meets its end in religious tradition because an uneducated self regulates the person, and self is naturally opposed to any challenging change or disposition. Without a faith purified by active involvement with salvation's science, the general devotional persuasion will be towards the natural logic of the body, and because the mind within the body lacks right sense, it will be fulfilled, "A deceived heart hath turned him aside, that he cannot deliver his soul, nor say, Is there not a lie in my right hand?"[415]

15. To get to our faith, and to help apprise us on the character of its *body*, the living God created a commandment for the resurrection and reformation of our inward parts, which is why it says, "Thou desirest truth in the inward parts: and in the hidden part thou shalt make me to know wisdom."[416] If the end of this commandment is "that we should be holy and without blame before him in love,"[417] it is that the conversation of the natural spiritual understanding, which contains no kind law or remedy for the mind within it, must find itself corrected and refreshed. With the conversation's conscience bound to a good commandment, the person may possess self to properly serve both its saving wisdom and other minds.

16. Our obedience to this commandment is the means whereby we may have knowledge to instruct the conversation's mind to better control self's thoughts and feelings, and this labor is the means whereby our faith is strengthened on the hope of the living God's will, making it well to experience this commandment's aim when our faith and spirit is young and innocent. There should be no thing stopping our mind from

---

414   1 Peter 1:18
415   Isaiah 44:20
416   Psalm 51:6
417   Ephesians 1:4

faithfully experimenting with the living God's sayings on "life," which is why we are counseled, "Be ye transformed by the renewing of your mind, that ye may prove what is that good, and acceptable, and perfect, will of God."[418]

17. Because "it is the spirit that quickeneth,"[419] it is absolutely crucial to our faith's learning that our mind receives personal knowledge of *creation's* science. Conversion of the heart and mind to the Bible's underlying philosophy is no mysterious happening, for by the understanding retained within the mind through proving the purpose behind the commandment, the mind is become the instrument used to convert the heart's organs to salvation's practice.

18. It is true that, if properly maintaining the devotional experience of the living God's chief apostle, the conversation will experience the same resurrection that his conversation received;[420] what must be quickened or regenerated are the members within the heart that are liable to pass away. The organs of our devotional faculties are to experience a resurrection in thought and in feeling, but in order to obtain this benevolence, the mind must consent to have the living God's wisdom existing within it, and this wisdom rests within the mind only by doing the Bible's commandment.

19. The force or substance of the living God's wisdom must enter into the mind if its will should find accomplishment within the person; if this commandment does not discipline the mind, we remove self from the opportunity to join into its kind intention. This wisdom's intention is the living God's manner of love, and if it says, "When Israel was a child, then I loved him,"[421] it is that our best chance to experience the intended tenderheartedness is when our faith is young. But a young faith means nothing if the heart will not quit its stubbornness to become teachable. Faith is retarded, and the mind is become degenerate, by fear and stubbornness.

---

418   Romans 12:2
419   John 6:63
420   Romans 8:11
421   Hosea 11:1

20. It is therefore well to intimately care for our faith's progress, for when faith reaches old age, it is very difficult to settle the heart to care for the revelation of *creation's* science. Old age is reached by failing to hear and do creation's law, for the end of the commandment is a clean spiritual understanding for perpetual knowledge of right affection. We should then know that "not the hearers of the law are just before God, but the doers of the law shall be justified."[422]

21. "Justification" is another name for "sanctification"; the two are one and the same; and if "this is the will of God, even your sanctification,"[423] and if "we might be justified by the faith of Christ,"[424] then it is crucial to our faith's age and growth that we learn of and do the living God's will and wisdom. Our conversation's conscience isn't cleansed or "justified" by a faith on a *man*; that is not what the Bible teaches; but our faith's mind is rather "sanctified" by the doctrine or knowledge of the living God's chief minister, which is why it says, "By his knowledge shall my righteous servant justify many."[425] Executing this knowledge prepares the way for our faith's sanctification to forward its development.

22. Faith's personal development is empty if ever found without sanctification's course of learning. "That which is born of the Spirit is spirit."[426] Our conversation must know that the *baptism* to occur is confined only to the spirit of the mind, and "that he might sanctify and cleanse it with the washing of water by the word."[427]

23. The mind must be cleansed of a false spiritual understanding. Our understanding of heavenly *things* must find itself washed by the instruction of "life's" commandment. This means that actual brain-power must be spent in order to comprehend the Bible's *voice*, which is why it says of the Bible's faithful, "His delight is in the law of the LORD; and in his law doth he meditate day and night."[428]

---

422 Romans 2:13
423 1 Thessalonians 4:3
424 Galatians 2:16
425 Isaiah 53:11
426 John 3:6
427 Ephesians 5:26
428 Psalm 1:2

24. Quiet meditation on the living God's words, apart from the noise of the religious world, will inform the mind of their intention. Should we care to own a strong and knowledgeable faith in the Bible's wisdom, a clean separation from the religious world, and a good effort to beat back self's impression of that *world*, is demanded. Paul, understanding the separation the person needs from their self and the *world* to commence their faith's higher learning, counsels, "Put off concerning the former conversation the old man...and be renewed in the spirit of your mind."[429]

25. The goal is to obtain the decreed newness from the Bible's present spiritual understanding, and this cannot take place when the mind is undecided. Either we will quit all religious *things* to freshly approach the Bible for its wisdom, or we will keep all *things* to renounce the promised recuperation confined to its wisdom's mediation.

26. The Bible's goal is not the religious world's ambition; the religious world has replaced faith's intelligent design with numbing policies "after the commandments and doctrines of men."[430] This is why the Bible counsels, "Love not the world, neither the things that are in the world...For all that is in the world, the lust of the flesh, and the lust of the eyes, and the pride of life, is not of the Father, but is of the world."[431]

27. Why should the religious world satisfy our faith? Doesn't the living God's chief messenger say, "I leave the world, and go to the Father"?[432] Doesn't this man's wisdom say, "For ever, O LORD, thy word is settled in heaven"?[433] Isn't it counsel, "Our conversation is in heaven"?[434] For what reason do we lower the Bible's standard?

28. Because our faith fails to reach into the *Temple* of the Bible's knowledge, the emptiness plaguing the *earth* has filled up our heart, causing us, being both spiritually hungry and thirsty, to wander through

---

429   Ephesians 4:22,23
430   Colossians 2:22
431   1 John 2:15,16
432   John 16:28
433   Psalm 119:89
434   Philippians 3:20

the *earth* for consolation. The end of an *earthy* conversation is famine, causing the person to overdose on theological prescriptions until their faith and mind pre-maturely passes away. But the living God's will, that we may know "a sound heart is the life of the flesh,"[435] is for our faith's higher education.

29. We should not waste our faith's youth, which is why we are counseled, "Walk not as other Gentiles walk, in the vanity of their mind, having the understanding darkened, being alienated from the life of God through the ignorance that is in them, because of the blindness of their heart."[436]

30. The practice created by the Bible's wisdom is wholly devoted to the will of that wisdom's throne, which is why it says, "Of his own will begat he us with the word of truth, that we should be a kind of first-fruits of his creatures."[437] With our mind fashioned after the heart of a child; honoring the character, "Criest after knowledge, and liftest up thy voice for understanding";[438] we will obtain permission to enter into the regeneration that is mentally and devotionally promised, making every principle in the Bible new to handle. It is this newness that opens up our understanding to the living God's operation, encouraging our heart to take and advance in the character surrounding the manner of creative love within the Bible.

31. When young in our heart of faith, when sincere in our intention to know the mystery of the Bible's doctrine, it is easier to simply pick up its words and learn for experiential knowledge, for then our faith's map may strengthen to direct our mind into our heart, and our heart into our mind, to convert their organs to stay on *creation's* saying. Our conversation's conscience is to perpetually experience the living God's pleasure. This pleasure is the means whereby our faith remains new and lively. We cannot risk weakening our faith by entertaining self-cultivated or inherited unbelief.

---

435   Proverbs 14:30
436   Ephesians 4:17,18
437   James 1:18
438   Proverbs 2:3

32. We are loved of the living God when simple in faith, therefore what is more important: the love of self and of the religious world, or the loving-kindness of the Bible's spiritual understanding? Knowledge of the Bible's science is not in self or within the religious world, which is why it says, "For ever, O LORD, thy word is settled in heaven."[439] If we are sincere, we will learn how to bring our faith into the *Place* where this wisdom is, for therein is the knowledge and wisdom of the Creator's justice.

33. Our faith is nourished and cared for by the Bible's *pleasure*, and this righteousness is an act that must be accomplished by the person cooperating with its wisdom, even as it says, "Every one that doeth righteousness is born of him,"[440] and, "If any man will do his will, he shall know of the doctrine,"[441] and, "Ye have purified your souls in obeying the truth through the Spirit."[442] It is our assignment to learn of and do "the doctrine which is according to godliness"[443] for the good of our faith. By interacting with this will, we have a sure opportunity to form and re-educate the body and organs of our heart and mind.

34. This is what matters, even the recovering and reforming of our lame mental and spiritual faculties. Our conversation is to become useful for this will's ministry, and since self and the religious world honor a desire contrary to its desire for personal and devotional well-being, it is well, if we care to be an epistle of its brilliance, to settle our person for learning how to possess self for the government of the mind and body. When our faith is young and our heart resembles the disposition of a child, the chance to know the living God's love increases, which edification alters the shape of our faith to encourage the honest transformation of our mind.

---

439   Psalm 119:89
440   1 John 2:29
441   John 7:17
442   1 Peter 1:22
443   1 Timothy 6:3

12

A Right Approach

1. When hopeful to understand any principle within the Bible, it is well to examine it not as one would examine a novel or a history book. It is true that the Bible contains many stories within it, but being "profitable for doctrine, for reproof, for correction, for instruction in righteousness,"[444] it is well to turn to the Bible in hope of profiting in what it educates on. Reading the Bible from firstly a literal or natural perspective will negatively disturb the mind.[445] Every *thing* in the Bible is formed around "the words which the LORD of hosts hath sent in his spirit by the former prophets,"[446] making it wrong to read the Bible through a firstly natural, historical, or human lens.

---

444   2 Timothy 3:16,17
445   1 Corinthians 2:14
446   Zechariah 7:12

2. If these words were uttered through a particular mind, then it is that, concerning every author of this volume, the saying is fulfilled, "He hath filled him with the spirit of God, in wisdom, in understanding, and in knowledge, and in all manner of workmanship."[447] The Bible's philosophy is the wisdom, understanding, and knowledge of creative devotional redemption; every book of the Bible serves to magnify the wisdom of this science. If we are not opening up the Bible with the intent of learning of and doing this wisdom, and if we are not observing those words through our mind, then with ordinary eyes we will behold the extraordinary, causing our heart to frustrate the Bible's sayings.

3. It is because we enter into the Bible's world with a natural mind that our understanding on spiritual things fails. The immediate reaction of most is to treat the Bible as literature that cannot be understood because it is literally irrational, and to the one naturally passing through it, it will appear so. Hate towards the Bible's mind is then mysteriously developed because the reader has failed to spend brainpower to discern the firstly philosophical understanding to secondly grasp the immediate. What is written in wisdom and by wisdom cannot be discerned unless through the devotional mind that it is written in, which is why it says, "Are ye so foolish? having begun in the Spirit, are ye now made perfect by the flesh?"[448]

4. Whosoever should pick up the Bible without accessing the spirit of their mind, seeing as how "that which is born of the Spirit is spirit,"[449] is in for a disappointment. Only the spirit of the mind, because "God is a Spirit,"[450] is ordained to understand scripture's *tongue*. That wisdom influencing the mind of *men* has structured the understanding of its Bible around the same *body* of knowledge, for "there is a natural body, and there is a spiritual body."[451] Now, "that was not first which is spiritual, but that which is natural; and afterward that which is spiritual";[452]

---

447 Exodus 35:31
448 Galatians 3:3
449 John 3:6
450 John 4:24
451 1 Corinthians 15:44
452 1 Corinthians 15:46

whosoever should care to comprehend the Bible's *voice*, it well for them to put off their natural mind to innocently put on the spiritual.

5. Our misunderstanding the Bible does not fall on the language of the Bible, but on us. Our natural reading of the Bible may produce discouragement or unbelief not for any thing done on the Bible's part, for it has guarded its understanding with cognitive prerequisites for the serious learner. It is because the conversation is not entirely sincere in its approach that it receives the rebuke, "God shall send them strong delusion, that they should believe a lie."[453]

6. "What shall we say then? Is there unrighteousness with God? God forbid."[454]

7. If we should think to clean our house, wouldn't we be mindful to prepare ourselves for the occasion? If we should think to attend a dinner party, wouldn't we be mindful to reorganize our thoughts and feelings for the event, even if we don't really care to attend, and to dress for the occasion? Would a mechanic wear his best clothes to work, or would he not think to dress for labor? If we were hungry, and our mind began to wonder about food, wouldn't we think to find food to satisfy our need? We wouldn't think to drink oil or to eat metal, but we would organize our thoughts around what nourishment our stomach either craves or delights in.

8. When opening the Bible, knowing that it is a book of philosophy ordained to forward a peculiar mental practice, must we not approach the Bible in the spirit of our mind above the impulse within our body? We should, which is why it says, "Worship God in the spirit."[455]

9. He or she not willing to put away their naturally sensual religious mind to approach the Bible with a heart free from preconceived notions drowned in theological lore will be kept from rightly comprehending the revelation of its wisdom. Like as swimming is only pleasurable in water, so also the *things* of the living God's mind are pleasurable

---

453 2 Thessalonians 2:11
454 Romans 9:14
455 Philippians 3:3

only to the spirit of the conversation's mind, which is why it says, "Be renewed in the spirit of your mind."[456]

10. This counsel directs the conversation to understand that the Bible is not simply a volume without beneficial and benevolent knowledge, but that it is to be blessed or edified by its content. The Bible "is profitable for doctrine, for reproof, for correction, for instruction in righteousness,"[457] and we are best cared for by its content if our heart and mind is open to receive correct knowledge of its doctrine to experience the kindness of its righteousness, which kindness is even "the mystery of his will, according to his good pleasure which he hath purposed in himself."[458]

11. With the heart determined to seek wisdom for its illness, or with the mind hopeful to correct its comprehension on the living God's *voice* to better apply self to that *voice*, reading the Bible no longer becomes a perplexing chore, but rather a pleasure to the mental faculties. I should not expect to understand one thing spoken by this book if my heart is not inclined to know the doctrine of its *pleasure*, which is why it says, "All the words of my mouth are in righteousness; there is nothing forward or perverse in them. They are all plain to him that understandeth, and right to them that find knowledge."[459]

12. If the Bible's will and wisdom is our desire, it is well to understand that rightly discerning any *thing* within it begins with our journey for knowing its *name*. When our heart can perceive "the knowledge of the Son of God,"[460] when our mind can appreciate "the law of the Spirit of life,"[461] then a free course will open up for grasping any and every principle within the Bible. Without personally understanding the law and knowledge of the Bible's wisdom, the Bible's language will appear to be weak, flatly contradicting, and without any value for the human mind.

----

456   Ephesians 4:23
457   2 Timothy 3:16
458   Ephesians 1:9
459   Proverbs 8:8,9
460   Ephesians 4:13
461   Romans 8:2

13. A natural reading of the Bible is injurious to the person because, seeing as how "God is a Spirit"[462] and "a spirit hath not flesh and bones,"[463] its *Author* is not natural. How then can flesh and bones understand what does not have its form, but is naturally contrary to it? Because the mind within the body is contrary to the mind within the Bible's devotional character,[464] it is no wonder why the sensual reader is turned away from the Bible, for "the natural man receiveth not the things of the Spirit of God."[465] And it is not just that the natural mind rejects the Bible's mind, but "they that are in the flesh cannot please God,"[466] for while the natural reader is frustrated because of the Bible's apparent ignorance, the mind within the Bible, due to their sensual approach, is hidden from them.

14. Because we all own a sorrow of heart familiar to us, it is no accident that we have picked up the Bible. The issue is not the content within this book, but rather the state of our heart when opening it up, along with the manner in which its *voice* is interpreted.

15. The Bible gives plain instructions for deciphering its wisdom, and this illustration, in order to consistently remain learning of its philosophy, is crucial for developing faith in the instruction of its commandment. To help us understand how to perceive its philosophy, "Precept must be upon precept, precept upon precept; line upon line, line upon line; here a little, and there a little,"[467] we are counseled. This method of study is for weighing one saying within one book of the Bible with another saying within that book, or with another saying in another book similar to the statement we examine, to better clarify what is being said.

16. An example would be comparing how it says, "Thy law is the truth,"[468] to how it says, "Thy word is truth,"[469] with how it says, "The

---

462   John 4:24
463   Luke 24:39
464   Galatians 5:17
465   1 Corinthians 2:14
466   Romans 8:8
467   Isaiah 28:10
468   Psalm 119:142
469   John 17:17

law is light."[470] We may draw many conclusions from these sayings, but when examining them together, we understand that the Bible's "word" is a "law of light," and when hearing, "God said, Let there be light: and there was light,"[471] by learning of what the Bible's "light" or "law" is, and by applying self to that "law," we may rightly discern creation's record to know that the Bible possesses a wisdom that "quickeneth the dead, and calleth those things which be not as though they were."[472] By carefully studying the Bible by the method of interpretation it gives, its language will become plain to our mind.

17. When reading the Bible as a history book or as a novel, we are examining its thoughts contrary to the method for edification. Without justly measuring one saying of the Bible with another, without "comparing spiritual things with spiritual,"[473] we will only find ourselves frustrated and inwardly agitated, for we are going against the ordained manner for mentally comprehending the Bible's language.

18. I will gain nothing from saying, "I will read the Bible and will start at Genesis," for what is my motivation to do so? My desire to know the *God* of the Bible, as innocent as it may be, cannot suffice for motivation to entertain something that is absent of sensuality.

19. Why then are we even reading the Bible? Why do we care to know the character within it? If I should say, "I will read the Bible, and will open up to Matthew, or to the Revelation, or to the book of Hebrews, and will not stop until I have read through Matthew, or the Revelation, or the book of Hebrews," for what reason do I put myself through that? What good is reading compared to learning? And what good is learning without a reason to learn? And what good is a reason to learn if not joined by faith in what we hope to learn? And what good is faith without understanding what to apply our heart to, and why?

20. There is a process attached to receiving confidence on the Bible's philosophy, and if we are not willing to consent to that process and its stages of personal devotional development, then we will not be

---

470 Proverbs 6:23
471 Genesis 1:3
472 Romans 4:17
473 1 Corinthians 2:13

allowed to know just what the Bible is saying. Instead of examining the Bible to get out of it what self is motivated to purge from it, open up the Bible to learn about how to soberly possess self through the *name* of the Bible's wisdom.

21. The Bible's philosophy is for benevolently possessing self's thoughts and feelings. There is no greater enemy that exists against the person than self. Every conversation drawn to the Bible, when the fashion of self is washed away and when the fear of the heart is cut off, will reveal a mind suffering some plight causing the person to abuse their heart or body. He or she turning to the Bible, whether or not they are conscious or unconscious of their heart's sorrow, is one praying, "I have borne chastisement, I will not offend any more: that which I see not teach thou me: if I have done iniquity, I will do no more."[474]

22. They have heard of the living God's chief apostle however they have heard of him, and there is something drawing them to know more about *creation's* act apart from self-cultivated or inherited religious tradition. For this cause, it is well to approach the Bible with an empty heart and mind, because if we hope to obtain a certain inward recovery from its words, must we ignore the condition of *earth* before it digested the Creator's voice?

23. The Bible's *voice* involves such a thorough mental and experimental investigation because we are to know that its wisdom is the only Creator in existence. When we come to its words without any form of understanding, being void of any knowledge on its *name*, and for opening up the Bible to learn of that *name*, we will experience the mystery of its understanding to acquire confidence on its wisdom's will.

24. This confidence motivates the person to consistently examine its words. Without a faith strengthened by knowledge, it will be impossible to value the Bible.[475] Thus, if actually desiring to open up this book for meaningfully reading it, it is that we must first have a developing faith on the intention of its wisdom.

---

474 Job 34:31,32
475 Hebrews 11:6

25. The conversation that is "flesh-based," or that would operate through theological assumptions on the Bible, cannot please the Bible's wisdom to pass into its higher learning because that wisdom only acknowledges an exercising of faith, and faith, if we should acknowledge it, must find itself verified and cultivated by "the acknowledging of the truth which is after godliness."[476] Our faith's training is based upon our willingness to learn of and do the Bible's words, which is why it says, "Ye have purified your souls in obeying the truth through the Spirit."[477]

26. Faith is activated by knowledge, and a desire for knowledge is activated by feelings or emotions, wherefore it well for the hopeful student of the Bible to know that "through desire a man, having separated himself, seeketh and intermeddleth with all wisdom."[478] Faith is cultivated and perfectly organized by mentally and physically doing the Bible's wisdom. Separation from self and the religious world is required if the mind should learn the Bible's science, for if the goal is to possess self, how is self to be understood when the heart is divided?[479]

27. Thus, there is a bit of an issue, because if I must first have a developing faith on the Bible's wisdom before I can meaningfully read it, how then can I, if having no faith developed in the Bible, read it? If I can only forward my understanding on the Bible's language by a cultivated faith on its *name*, how then am I to go about understanding its words without any faith cultivated on that *name*?

28. The answer: How we present our mind to the mind within the Bible's wisdom matters.

29. Every conversation outside of the Bible's course of learning is naturally foreign to its language and does sensually honor some perversion of its context, but then there are minds that truly desire knowledge on how to rightly benefit from its philosophy who, after years of personal and devotional abuse, pray, "I am ready to halt, and my

---

476   Titus 1:1
477   1 Peter 1:22
478   Proverbs 18:1
479   Luke 11:17

sorrow is continually before me. For I will declare mine iniquity; I will be sorry for my sin."[480]

30. Such a mind will take their faith's confidence and learn how to humble their heart for knowledge. Having only a hope of being delivered from spiritual sickness, these pick up the Bible and simply read not to read, but they read to be read by words. We then gain faith on the Bible only as we personally handle its instruction, and by learning of and applying self to its *diet*, our mental and devotional experience will develop an intelligent faith that is based on what is proven.

31. Our experimental faith is the means whereby we have confidence, and are comfortable to learn, from the Bible. If the state of our heart is framed towards the issue in our heart, then wherever we turn to in the Bible will unseal to us a remedy for our conflict.

32. The Bible's course of learning, to the end we may better care for that wisdom, self, and other minds, is for cleansing and reestablishing the government of our faith's heart. If our heart is set on being healed, then our time in the Bible will not be with a book, but with a love letter confessing a remedy for our thoughts and feelings. As we take note of this letter, carefully digesting its contents and letting that sustenance rejuvenate the organs of our inward person, confidence to further learn of the Bible's will, to benefit from the intercession of its wisdom, will keep the heart warm for the reception of its regenerating influence.

33. This wisdom will never turn away a broken heart. It will never reject any one who is humbly willing to quit self for recovering self, even as it says, "The LORD is nigh unto them that are of a broken heart; and saveth such as be of a contrite spirit."[481] Herein is the key to receiving a seat in the Bible's classroom, and it is the state of the spirit of our heart and mind when approaching its words.

34. A broken mind will not care about any *thing* but wholeness, and concerning every *thing* that mind must endure for sobriety, it is counted as a sweet delight, for its eye of faith sees the end of a great

---

480   Psalm 38:17,18
481   Psalm 34:18

mystery. Thus, one's faith and mind work together to create a new heart within the person, for this new mind is the means whereby love to the Bible's philosophy is strengthened, and it is known that "wisdom strengtheneth."[482]

35. Because the wisdom of *creation's* science fails to meet the heart of the Bible's casual or surface reader, many are turned away, or are reliant upon a traditional prescription for a satisfactory form of devotion. Due to their approach, because they have no knowledgeable motivation to know the living God, or no contrite disposition to receive correction from the Bible's words to keep their *eyes* heavenward, they should be and remain turned away. The living God's intention for our conversation is not carnal or sensual. The Bible intends to give our faith an absolutely phenomenal gift within the conscience of its conversation, but in order to receive it, we must need what it is offering.

---

482   Ecclesiastes 7:19

13

Built Up and Restored

1. The conversation hearing and acknowledging the Bible's present mind, and actively exercising faith on that philosophy, is given a revival of heart and mind from which it will never, if willing to embrace humility to become teachable, know reproach.[483] If we will allow our hearts to be convicted by the power of the Bible's words, soon our conversion will positively manifest itself through a sound mind.

2. From lifting up the standard to enter into such a blessing, the heart will no longer remain cold to right benevolence but will, with the *life* given it through the Bible's words, strengthen every fiber of the conversation's character to desire to do right by others and by the living God's words. As long as the conversation reverences what it acquires from doing the Bible's philosophy, keeping every remembrance of service to the living God within its mind, it will know no *death*, or no

---

483   Proverbs 1:33

heartache over the correction given within its experience with the Bible. We are, by faith on the knowledge gained, to take hold of the living God's promises.

3. Obedience to the kind philosophy within the Bible yields peaceable *fruit* due to its development of an honorable conversation, but it is presumption that governs a false experience with the Bible. Presumption is an experience fueled by feeling, and when temperament becomes the source of motivation, as if a controlling power to perform the active forms of religion without a living principle for human growth and development, a contrary character controls the experience. Submission to conventional practices, whether traditional or superstitious, will reserve the conversation for decay, leading to injury through appetite.[484]

4. Our experience in the Bible is for a revival of our conversation's thoughts and feelings. By cooperating with the influence that the Bible's words give to our devotional confidence, we will learn of and live its counsels. "Durable riches and righteousness"[485] are freely given to the conversation willing to cancel self-sufficiency. Thus, "Whoso findeth me findeth life,"[486] says the Bible's wisdom, "and shall obtain favour."[487] Hereafter it is said of the conversation willing to learn the Bible's present will and wisdom, "The LORD hath loved him."[488]

5. The living God is the Creator of conversations daily striving to honor the saying, "Put off concerning the former conversation the old man...and be renewed in the spirit of your mind."[489] Because we have perseveringly sought to know the Bible's present wisdom, our conversation will grow in health. Our effort to better our faith must then be diligently guarded against, and because it is not ultimately in our own power to live justly, because it is not natural for our conversation to will and to do according to the Bible's mind, how much more respect for the living God's grace ought we to have?

---

484   1 Peter 1:18
485   Proverbs 8:18
486   Proverbs 8:35
487   Proverbs 8:35
488   Isaiah 48:14
489   Ephesians 4:22,23

6. Our faith's first assignment is to have an intelligent faith, and the reason being is that, a correct conversation cannot be achieved if we have not first sought out a pure understanding while possessing an imperfect conversation. *Death*, or our inability to understand the Bible's mind, cannot be swallowed up in victory if we have not allowed our life to be devoured by what appears to be failure. How then can we ever know that our failure is met with *unforeseen* strength?

7. If we fail to see the need to recover our faith's character, and even overlook the fact that only an exercised faith on what the living God's chief counselor taught can properly guide our training, then we fail to accept the conditions for edification; this is what causes the heart to harden in religious stubbornness. But let it rather be understood, "The fear of the LORD tendeth to life: and he that hath it shall abide satisfied; he shall not be visited with evil."[490]

8. The living God's wisdom is what adds knowledge to our conversation for bettering our living experience. With what we learn daily exercised, the faith we develop in the Bible's words will purify our intention to not only know them, but to know the Mind that inspired them. There is a reason, then, why it says of our faith's guide, "In him was life; and the life was the light of men."[491] From what he taught, his words revived many conversations to experience a more complete relationship with both *life* and *life's* Creator.

9. There is no natural desire within us to know the Bible's will and wisdom. Yet should we allow the Bible into our life, should we learn and exercise its sayings, something unnatural will happen: we will care to know the Bible's mind, to experiment with it. This experimentation is the means whereby our character gains development through discipline, which discipline is for creating within us a faith that is genuine to our person. It is the living God's grace that will turn presumption into an intelligent and godly inclination.

10. *Creation's* present law and science comes to us through the illustration of the crucifixion, teaching, "He that raised up Christ from

---

490   Proverbs 19:23
491   John 1:4

the dead shall also quicken your mortal bodies by his Spirit that dwelleth in you."[492] No longer will old *things* cause us to stumble. In spirit and in truth we receive the hidden commandment within that illustration and by faith we are given showers of blessing that we may prove it. Hereafter our conversation, being "filled with the knowledge of his will in all wisdom and spiritual understanding,"[493] will be the sufficiency for our human being.

11. Without the living God's refreshing showers of blessing convicting and correcting our faith's mind, our conversation cannot know the Bible's intention for it. Only by the substance of grace can we maintain the conversation of the living God's chief apostle. We get grace to apply to our mind as we consistently review the Bible's words. This is why it says, "Grace and peace be multiplied unto you through the knowledge of God."[494]

12. The living God has given our faith a diet. "We have received a commandment from the Father."[495] Without eating or meditating on what the living God has given to us, which is a saying for our conversation to know, we will not receive edifying showers to properly order our experience.

13. We receive, from out of the Creator's presence, *rain* to help prosper our faith's *fruit*, that by faithfully accepting the Bible as our main source of learning, we can know and experience the living God's intended kindness. This is why it says, "My doctrine shall drop as the rain."[496]

---

492   Romans 8:11
493   Colossians 1:9
494   2 Peter 1:2
495   2 John 1:4
496   Deuteronomy 32:2

14

A Covenant of Peace

1. Turing to the parable within the book of Galatians, it is written, "Abraham had two sons, the one by a bondmaid, the other by a free-woman. But he who was of the bondwoman was born after the flesh; but he of the freewoman was by promise. Which things are an allegory; for these are two covenants; the one from mount Si'nai, which gendereth to bondage, which is A'gar."[497]

2. By such an example, Paul contrasts the experience of a mind under that covenant from the Mosaic dispensation with a conversation under the present devotional promise. While one experience is categorized as being binding, in that the mind is trained to grow accustomed to a form of religious slavery, the other experience is liberating, in that the son of the freewoman represents the experience of a mind able to freely think and feel on how it relates to its faith, to

---

497   Galatians 4:22-24

its devotional experience, and to the scriptures. With no other mind or conscience outside of its own suppressing its expression, the liberated experience can have its peace, while the experience bound by regulation will never know a sincere and edifying manner of devotion.

3. The "flesh" that Paul mentions should not be taken literally. Paul, though speaking figuratively, is touching on two ways one's faith can exist. The first way is through heavily relying upon one's "flesh," or upon one's conversation, as being a means whereby their faith is carried out and understood. Executing our faith in this way prevents a genuine exercising of love, of curiosity, of creativity, and of learning from taking place. Concerning such a conversation, Paul stimulates thought on its injury to our conversation by saying, "Why is my liberty judged of another man's conscience."[498]

4. The second way to manage our faith is be refraining from relying upon our "flesh," or upon the stimulus given through the *body* of our belief. Such a conversation honors the saying, "Be transformed by the renewing of your mind, that ye may prove what is that good, and acceptable, and perfect, will of God."[499]

5. That second way to manage our faith places us in remembrance of how it says, "That was not first which is spiritual, but that which is natural; and afterward that which is spiritual.[500] This thought moves the mind to think on the first covenant, how it greatly relied upon the actions of the conversation for relevance. It was this covenant that forwarded the referenced "bondage," keeping the mind natural or flesh-based in how it approached and thought on the living God. Concerning such a ministry, Paul calls it, "The ministration of death."[501]

6. It is the ministration of death because, through a dead devotional practice or approach, such as maintaining belief on *God* through rituals, sacrifices, ordinances, traditions, theories, and baptisms, the individual keeps their faith asleep. Contrary to this experience is "the

---

498   1 Corinthians 10:29
499   Romans 12:2
500   1 Corinthians 15:46
501   2 Corinthians 3:7

ministration of the spirit,"[502] where the conversation is able to personally discover and experience the beauty of its character by taking knowledge of the Bible's words. Such a conversation is advised: "Be renewed in the spirit of your mind."[503]

7. The practice given at Si'nai was fulfilled through works that bound the "flesh," or the conversation, to perform what was written, and that without a sure remedy of deliverance from personal and devotional error for justification. The only good that came from this activity was that the works, without actually delivering a refreshed heart and mind, served to stir up hope for a new heart and mind within the remorseful. This is why Paul, because it is but a show of unjust regard for self, criticizes such a demonstration of faith, saying that it "could not make him that did the service perfect, as pertaining to the conscience."[504]

8. It is written of the duty to this covenant, "I gave them my statutes, and showed them my judgments, which if a man do, he shall even live in them."[505] Again, "They walked not in my statutes, and they despised my judgments, which if a man do, he shall live in them."[506] And once more, "The children rebelled against me: they walked not in my statutes, neither kept my judgments to do them, which if a man do, he shall even live in them."[507] This covenant was binding upon the conscience, forcefully dictating to the person their conversation's character, yet the new covenant states, "I will put my spirit within you, and cause you to walk."[508]

9. Our conversation is called to honor the living God through the ministration of the spirit, or through a mind set on learning the living God's *name* by taking personal knowledge of that *name*. To the

---

502 2 Corinthians 3:8
503 Ephesians 4:23
504 Hebrews 9:9
505 Ezekiel 20:11
506 Ezekiel 20:13
507 Ezekiel 20:21
508 Ezekiel 36:27

conversation willing to take responsibility for its interaction with its own character, it will be said, "He liveth unto God."[509]

10. The illustration of the living God's chief apostle being crucified teaches us that the former way to approach *God* is passed away. This is why it says, "Even so we also should walk in newness of life."[510] Being passed away, the conversation is free from it. Being free from it, the conversation is resurrected in thought and in feeling, approaching the living God "in newness of spirit, and not in the oldness of the letter."[511] This means that, having a conversation bound by no religious law, we have the opportunity to freely learn of and experiment with the principles of the living God's character.

11. To turn from an experience based upon presumption means to become convinced of the living God's words over and within the human being, yet if not discerning that doctrine, the Bible's words will never be understood. Because the heart refuses to be convinced, the mind is told by the heart to decree its own rules and regulations, placing a complete block on the mind for revelation, causing the living God's mind to withdraw from the experience. Soon we will search out means to understand the Bible apart from that mind within the Bible, declaring of the voices within the religious world, "Hear all that the LORD our God shall say; and speak thou unto us all that the LORD our God shall speak unto thee; and we will hear it, and do it."[512]

12. Such a profession is a mockery of the intended Bible experience. The living God communes with our faith for edifying it; edification is a gift to the conversation sincerely inquiring of *heavenly things*. Our only means for understanding the Bible is to search through the mind that inspired it. This experience is indeed a great gift, because by putting our mind to use, we grow fond of wrong religious habits, and of right devotional habits, and of the living God's science.

13. The Bible is concerned with our faith's intellectual and philosophical growth, and as we are joined to its mind, not only will our

---

509   Romans 6:10
510   Romans 6:4
511   Romans 7:6
512   Deuteronomy 5:27

mind develop, but also a truehearted and tenderhearted conversation will be returned to us. When clearly observing the living God's benevolence, our conversation's character is truly changed into its very *image* for an inward stillness that is unmatched.

15

The Former Covenant

1. The living God's new covenant promise is for separating the conversation's thoughts and feelings from an *earthy* experience, seeing as how it says, "As is the earthy, such are they also that are earthy."[513] Thus, as was previously thought, and is still faithlessly observed, "If the ministration of condemnation be glory, much more doth the ministration of righteousness exceed in glory."[514]

2. The mind that has not experienced the living God's benevolence will not care for the promises of the new covenant. Concerning that new promise, it says, "The last Adam was made a quickening spirit,"[515] meaning that the conversation willing to spend time with its self, to know its character through growing familiar with the living God's

---

513   1 Corinthians 15:48
514   2 Corinthians 3:9
515   1 Corinthians 15:45

devotional mind, will also be quickened, or resurrected, or regenerated. This is why it says, "Be ye not unwise, but understanding what the will of the Lord is."[516]

3. When referencing the covenant given to ancient Israel, we read it to have been written according to how it says, "It be but a man's covenant."[517] Seeing as how a "man" is but flesh, that first covenant must be accomplished through the body. Such a covenant, being linked to "man," is then understood from how it says, "Man is like to vanity,"[518] and, "Verily every man at his best state is altogether vanity."[519]

4. The former covenant was a covenant of vanity. But how so? It is written, "Men verily swear by the greater: and an oath for confirmation is to them an end of all strife."[520] And again, as spoken by Nehemiah, "I called the priests, and took an oath of them, that they should do according to this promise."[521] Being driven by "oath," and by the will of the body, with the mind playing no major part in the experience, this covenant is weak.

5. We may also look at this covenant as being driven by *God* not for any sure intent, but simply for his faithfulness to Abraham, to Isaac, and to Jacob. This is why it says, "Because he loved thy fathers, therefore he chose their seed after them,"[522] and, "Because the LORD loved you, and because he would keep the oath which he had sworn unto your fathers, hath the LORD brought you out with a mighty hand, and redeemed you."[523]

6. The "covenant he made with Abraham, and his oath unto Isaac,"[524] *God* "confirmed the same unto Jacob for a law, and to Israel for an everlasting covenant."[525] The covenant made anciently was made

---

516 Ephesians 5:17
517 Galatians 3:15
518 Psalms 144:4
519 Psalms 39:5
520 Hebrews 6:16
521 Nehemiah 5:12
522 Deuteronomy 4:37
523 Deuteronomy 7:8
524 Psalm 105:9
525 Psalm 105:10

because of the love and respect wherewith *God* had for Abraham, and because their *God* is faithful and will not break his own promise, *God* chose Israel. But there is a greater reason as to why this covenant is vain, and it has to do with the fact that it was held together by a certain spoken promise.

7. According to the Bible, a covenant is a "league." A "league" is a deal that is formed through swearing or through an oath. The definition of a "league" is further understood from how it says, "My covenant will I not break, nor alter the thing that is gone out of my lips."[526] A covenant, or a league, an agreement by oath or by swearing, is a promise which is gone out of the lips, therefore the old covenant with Israel is a covenant which was only spoken, and we but need find the spoken words of the covenant to prove what that covenant was.

8. It says, in the book of Judges, "Ye have not obeyed my voice: why have ye done this?"[527] Israel broke the league, or the covenant that they had made with *God* not simply by breaking the Ten Commandments, not by violating any of the other commandments or ordinances imposed on them, but by disobeying the charge initially connected to their *God's voice*.

9. From how it says, "They went a whoring after other gods, and bowed themselves unto them: they turned quickly out of the way which their fathers walked in, obeying the commandments of the LORD; but they did not so,"[528] we see that this *voice* wasn't enough to keep them faithful. Because it was a flesh-based covenant, there was nothing more that *God* could have done for them. Herein we are turned to that covenant, in that it said, "If ye will obey my voice indeed, and keep my covenant, then ye shall be a peculiar treasure unto me above all people."[529] "And all the people answered together, and said, All that the LORD hath spoken we will do. And Moses returned the words of the people unto the LORD."[530]

---

526   Psalms 89:34
527   Judges 2:2
528   Judges 2:17
529   Exodus 19:5
530   Exodus 19:8

10. To reiterate, this covenant states: "Obey my voice. Obey my voice in diligence and in truth, and keep my covenant, which covenant is this that I now make with you presently, saying, Obey my voice. The covenant is that by diligently obeying my voice, you will in turn receive blessings peculiar only to you on the face of this earth. Should you observe to obey my voice only, you will not break this covenant between me and you, which covenant is this, that you have agreed to obey my voice."

11. The covenant of old was an agreement to obey all of *God's* words, and to do them, to the end that "he will love thee, and bless thee, and multiple thee,"[531] said Moses. "He will also bless the fruit of thy womb, and the fruit of thy land, thy corn, and thy wine, and thine oil, the increase of thy kine, and of the flocks of thy sheep, in the land which he sware unto thy fathers to give thee. Thou shalt be blessed above all people,"[532] he added.

12. Again, it was said, "It shall come to pass, if ye shall hearken diligently unto my commandments which I command you this day, to love the LORD your God, and to serve him with all your heart and with all your soul, that I will give you the rain of your land in his due season, the first rain and the latter rain, that thou mayest gather in thy corn, and thy wine, and thine oil. And I will send grass in thy fields for thy cattle, that thou mayest eat and be full. Take heed to yourselves, that your heart be not deceived, and ye turn aside, and serve other gods, and worship them."[533]

13. This is why *God* ended up telling them, "Cursed be the man that obeyeth not the words of this covenant."[534] But what words? These are the words: "Thou hast avouched the LORD this day to be thy God, and to walk in his ways, and to keep his statutes, and his commandments, and his judgments, and to hearken unto his voice: and the LORD hath

---

531 Deuteronomy 7:13
532 Deuteronomy 7:13
533 Deuteronomy 11:13-16
534 Jeremiah 11:3

avouched thee this day to be a peculiar people, as he hath promised thee, and that thou shouldest keep all his commandments."[535]

14. These are the words of the covenant, or of the league made anciently, to swear to hear and keep all that comes out from *God*. Yet the *Lord* continues by Jeremiah: "I commanded your fathers in the day that I brought them forth out of the land of Egypt, from the iron furnace, saying, Obey my voice, and do them, according to all which I command you: so shall ye be my people, and I will be your God."[536]

15. The covenant of old said, "Israel, abide by my voice, keep my sayings, so shall you prosper." And it was completed by Israel saying, "Lord, we hear you and will do all things that come out of your mouth." Once the covenant was sealed and both parties were in agreement, then *God* spoke from out of the fire, declaring to them the words that they were to keep, *writing* them in stone.[537]

16. The Ten Commandments aren't the old covenant. The two tables of the league are the words they had sworn to honor even before officially hearing what those words were. These commandments were given them to perform. The words on these two tables are the words of the covenant and not the covenant itself, or are the words of the agreement that they, to the end they may be *God's* official priesthood, were to obey. After receiving these words, Moses then places the assembly in remembrance of the covenant that they had sworn to keep, saying, "Ye shall observe to do therefore as the LORD your God hath commanded you: ye shall not turn aside to the right hand or to the left. Ye shall walk in all the ways which the LORD your God hath commanded you, that ye may live, and that it may be will with you, and that ye may prolong your days in the land which ye shall possess."[538]

17. The commandments that they received were not the covenant. These words were the means by which the covenant was to be perfectly regulated, as is a society regulated and kept in order by the laws of which it abides. The "league," then, between the individual and

---

535   Deuteronomy 26:17,18
536   Jeremiah 11:4
537   Deuteronomy 4:11-14
538   Deuteronomy 5:32,33

society is not the laws that regulate them, but the expected promise to be a lawful citizen through society's code of conduct. Placed into this context, ought we to call that "code" the "league," or ought we not to call our solemnly swearing to uphold that "code" the "league" in reference?

18. For this cause it is written, "I was gone up into the mount to receive the tables of stone, even *the tables of the covenant* which the LORD made with you,"[539] and, "The LORD gave me the two tables of stone, even *the tables of the covenant*,"[540] and, "The LORD delivered unto me two tables of stone written with the finger of God; and on them was written according *to all the words*, which the LORD spake with you in the mount out of the midst of the fire."[541]

19. The doing of these words confirmed these people as *God's* people. To violate the covenant would not only mean to violate the words of the covenant, but it would ultimately mean to violate the oath that was taken before these words of the covenant were actually given. That covenant which Israel swore over was a "deal" to simply keep the commandments that *God* told them to keep.

---

539   Deuteronomy 9:9
540   Deuteronomy 9:11
541   Deuteronomy 9:10

16

The Ministration of The Spirit

1. Seeing how that neither *God's* ten precepts, nor the laws concerning health, nor the statutes and judgments, nor his testimonies, nor the other ordinances and customs imposed on Israel actually constituted the old covenant, but rather the covenant was a simple oath concerning obedience to *God's voice*, which *voice* came after the two parties agreed to the deal, we can now see how truly insufficient this first covenant was. Although confirmed by blood[542] and surrounded by terrible majesty,[543] this covenant lacked one thing, and that one thing is "not by might, nor by power, but by my spirit, saith the LORD."[544]

2. The old covenant lacked the movement of the living God's indwelling presence to seal the conversation's character with *his*

---

542   Exodus 24:8
543   Exodus 19:16
544   Zechariah 4:6

devotional character. The foundation of the new covenant is that "I will put my law in their inward parts, and write it in their hearts."[545] How so? It says, "Jesus stooped down, and with his finger wrote on the ground."[546]

3. Those ten precepts of the first covenant are to be sealed within the heart of our conversation through the promise of the new covenant. This is to take place as we cooperate "with the finger of God."[547] The promise is: "A new heart also will I give you, and a new spirit will I put within you: and I will take away the stony heart out of your flesh, and I will give you an heart of flesh. And I will put my spirit within you, and cause you to walk,"[548] and, "Ye shall be my people, and I will be your God,"[549] and, "They shall know me."[550]

4. The old covenant was given without the hope of the Creator's sealing and teaching power. It was given without a sure route to that hope of having the knowledge of the love of *God* within the soul, but was administered by faith in hope that the people would gain that knowledge through outward works. The former ministration was established on the grounds of obedience to his *voice* and this has not changed. But at this time, we have full confidence that better promises are given to us for honoring that *voice*, which voice was imperfectly kept through a routine of religious laws.[551]

5. Because of God's terrible *sight*, the people exclaimed, "Why should we die? For this great fire will consume us: if we hear the voice of the LORD our God any more, then shall we die."[552] Yet the same fire that dwelt on the mount is that same fire that is to keep our conversation devoted to the words of the present covenant. This is why it says, "Who among us shall dwell with the devouring fire?"[553]

---

545   Jeremiah 31:33
546   John 8:6
547   Luke 11:20
548   Ezekiel 36:26,27
549   Jeremiah 30:22
550   Jeremiah 31:34
551   Hebrews 10:1,2; Hebrews 9:9.10
552   Deuteronomy 5:25
553   Isaiah 33:14

6. Today, the living God can detect the true and right conversation. Anciently, it was that if you do all of the words that were spoken, and however you should physically do them, you should be well. Presently, it is that if the conversation can become teachable, allowing the spirit of its mind to regenerate through the words of the Bible's present *voice*, that *voice* will write upon our faith's thoughts and feelings every commandment of the living God. Hereafter it is well to know that the living God "hath in these last days spoken unto us by his Son."[554]

7. Not only do we now have the Creator's *influence* as our educator, as that agent convicting our heart on all matters concerning our faith, as well as on injurious practices for our conversation, it is also written, "They shall teach no more every man his neighbour, and every man his brother, saying, Know the LORD: for they shall all know me, from the least of them unto the greatest of them, saith the LORD."[555] Thus, concerning that former covenant, "that which decayeth and waxeth old is ready to vanish away"[556] that we may come to personally know the living God.

8. The ministration of the spirit of our faith's mind is of "a greater and more perfect tabernacle,"[557] and is not reduced to religious vanity, but rather this ministration is a real and everlasting reality. There is presently, for our conversation's consolation, a *light* added to the Ten Commandments, even like as it says, "A law shall proceed from me, and I will make my judgment to rest for a light of the people."[558] This "law" is the present *voice* or philosophy of the Bible for the conversation's wellbeing.

9. The present *light* or *voice* of the living God is given to do what the flesh could not do under the former covenant. The routine to please *God* by religious laws is passed away, this *light* or "law" replacing it. Thus, "if that which is done away was glorious, much more that which

---

554   Hebrews 1:2
555   Jeremiah 31:34
556   Hebrews 8:13
557   Hebrews 9:11
558   Isaiah 51:4

remaineth is glorious,"[559] "for the law made nothing perfect, but the bringing in of a better hope did; by the which we draw night unto God."[560]

10. The Bible is clear. The former covenant, in order to keep the Ten Commandments, was kept through religious laws. These laws, being weak in that they did not transform the conscience, did nothing but pervert the experience. But the living God, that our conversation may not fail where the ancient conversation failed, has left us a "law" and an "example" to mirror.

11. Honoring the "blood" of the living God's chief apostle, we will come to know the *light* that he spoke. This "blood" is not literal blood. We are not to be thought of as vampires, or to force literal blood into possessing a meaning not intended by the Bible. "The life of the flesh is in the blood,"[561] and because the body of our conversation is to be the subject of the new covenant promise, this "blood" must not be thought of as being literal blood, and must not be taken to mean what the Bible's does not say of it.

12. This "blood," in plain language, is one's struggle to apply that *voice* to the personal and the devotional conversation. Our "life," or our inspiration for caring to maintain a thoughtful conversation, comes from "blood," making it well to hear how it says, "The excellency of knowledge is, that wisdom giveth life to them that have it."[562] Thus, while the Bible may use colorful language, such as "blood," to articulate its philosophy, the fact of the matter is that the "blood" in reference is the implementation of a specific "wisdom" or "knowledge."[563]

13. Accepting and growing familiar with this *blood*, or with an experience in this *knowledge*, is the means whereby the new covenant promise is fulfilled.[564] And so we see that the former covenant was ratified with blood, and that literal blood doing nothing for the mind. Yet

---

559   2 Corinthians 3:11
560   Hebrews 7:19
561   Leviticus 17:11
562   Ecclesiastes 7:12
563   Ephesians 4:13
564   Romans 3:21-25

the new covenant with *blood*, or with a course of learning that is able to inwardly perform more than what was once thought to be *divine*. This is truly good and revolutionary news for our conversation, because if willing to patiently and temperately examine the Bible's words, and for knowledge of that inwardly working "wisdom," the flow of our devotion to the living God will appear as natural as breathing does to the body.

14. The foundation of the old and new covenant is of similar background, yet the foundation of the new being founded upon better promises for a more reliable outcome. The blood of the old covenant decreed no such justice towards the conscience of conversations seeking an honest experience, yet while confirmed by blood, it was to last only until an appointed time. This former covenant was sufficient "for the time then present,"[565] but now we have been given a higher learning, which training is "not of blood, nor of the will of the flesh, nor of the will of man, but of God."[566]

15. Knowing the present *voice* within the Bible is our conversation's first responsibility. When entered into the realm of Bible religions, we enter enthusiastically, yet somehow, if our faith is not cared for, we grow lazy in comfortable and stimulating religious theories. The living God has instituted a higher learning for our faith so that our conversation may recover its senses. Hereafter our first thought should be, "That I may know him,"[567] and, "Found in him, not having my own righteousness, which is of the law, but that which is through the faith of Christ, the righteousness which is of God by faith."[568]

---

565 Hebrews 9:9
566 John 1:13
567 Philippians 3:10
568 Philippians 3:9

17

Faith's Stand

1. "The steps of a good man are ordered by the LORD: and he delighteth in his way. Though he fall, he shall not be utterly cast down: for the LORD upholdeth him with his hand."[569] "For a just man falleth seven times, and riseth up again: but the wicked shall fall in mischief."[570] Yet "like as a father pitieth his children, so the LORD pitieth them that fear him. For he knoweth our frame; he remembereth that we are dust."[571]

2. "Surely it is meet to be said unto God, I have borne chastisement, I will not offend any more: that which I see not teach thou me: if I have done iniquity, I will do no more."[572] "Herein do I exercise myself, to have always a conscience void of offence toward God, and

---

569   Psalms 37:23,24
570   Psalms 24:16
571   Psalms 103:13,14
572   Job 34:31,32

toward men,"[573] "in that he saith, A new covenant."[574] "I will put my laws into their mind, and write them in their hearts: and I will be to them a God, and they shall be to me a people...I will be merciful to their unrighteousness, and their sins and their iniquities will I remember no more."[575]

3. The issue of personal devotional error, seeing as how there was "a remembrance again made of sins every year,"[576] was not correctly handled under the first covenant. Our conversation is no longer held to an experience where inward, religious, and theological deviation tarnishes it, which is why it says, "But now we are delivered from the law, that being dead wherein we were held; that we should serve in newness of spirit."[577]

4. The conversation's righteousness, under the former covenant, was achieved through doing, believing on, and acting out religious laws. The former covenant was fraudulent because it is wrong to believe that physical acts, or that a belief on religious theories, is enough to bless the conversation. A "surface" or "nominal" religious experience is held to the doing and demonstration of commandments, rituals, theories, and rites, but under the new covenant, which is a promise of transformation for the conversation's thoughts and feelings, such an experience is categorized by the Bible as "sin," even like as it says, "The strength of sin is the law."[578]

5. Paul, in the book of Galatians, uses the story of Isaac's birth to articulate this fact. It is written of old, "Sarah saw the son of Ha'gar the Egyptian, which she had born unto Abraham, mocking."[579] That "mocking" son represents a religious philosophy mocking at or scoffing its observer, even like as it says, "That could not make him that did the service perfect, as pertaining to the conscience."[580]

---

573   Acts 24:16
574   Hebrews 8:13
575   Hebrews 8:10-12
576   Hebrews 10:3
577   Romans 7:6
578   1 Corinthians 15:56
579   Genesis 21:9
580   Hebrews 9:9

6. The first covenant mocks the intelligence of the human being's faith. How? Just think: if "God is a Spirit,"[581] and if "a spirit hath not flesh and bones,"[582] ought we to think that our flesh and blood service is blessed or condoned by what has no flesh and blood? The conversation given to religious theories and commandments, to baptisms, traditions, commandments, and rites, is a conversation undermining the fact of faith, that only a mental and inward sacrifice is key to achieving the intended blessing. This is why it says, "I desired mercy, and not sacrifice; and the knowledge of God more than burnt offerings,"[583] and, "If righteousness come by the law, then Christ is dead in vain."[584]

7. The covenant of old was temporary and binding, for it says, "I took my staff, even Beauty, and cut it asunder, that I might break my covenant which I had made with all the people."[585] The Bible is plain: a new manner to carry the conversation should exist, replacing the former manner. Hereafter every faithful experience should reflect the saying, "By his knowledge shall my righteous servant justify man."[586]

8. It is written, "Strength and beauty are in his sanctuary."[587] *God* took his "Beauty," or that *thing* supposedly reflecting his glory, and delivered "his glory into the enemy's hands,"[588] even into the hands of "Herod, and Pon'tius Pilate, with the Gentiles, and the people of Israel."[589] This is why it says, "Christ hath redeemed us from the curse of the law."[590]

9. Today, "sin" is defined as carrying the conversation according to former religious thought and process. The "fame" of the former covenant, which gave *righteousness* to the individual through "meats and drinks, and divers washings, and carnal ordinances, imposed,"[591]

---

581   John 4:24
582   Luke 24:39
583   Hosea 6:6
584   Galatians 2:21
585   Zechariah 11:10
586   Isaiah 53:11
587   Psalms 96:6
588   Psalm 78:61
589   Acts 4:27
590   Galatians 3:12
591   Hebrews 9:10

is dead, its death figuratively illustrated through the crucifixion of the living God's chief apostle. Hereafter our mind becomes the greatest offering to the living God and "our conversation is in heaven,"[592] "unto the city of the living God, the heavenly Jerusalem."[593]

10. Instead of being mindful to a *dead* devotional approach, the Bible advises us to become alive to the present course of learning. Instead of remaining faithful to a form of worship the Bible states as being abolished, we ought to give our minds to the accepted dispensation.

11. A love for the living God is presently lacking. A love for Bible is lacking. Knowledge of the intended Bible experience is unknown. Pride in a useless and clearly rejected religious operation is preventing benevolent self-reflection for kind self-regulation. The result is that our conversation, while thinking to know what it believes, until willing to let go of its handwritten approach, is yet failing, groping in the dark, even like as it says, "They grope in the dark without light."[594]

12. The spirit of the mind, and not the impulse of the body, is to guide the conversation. "He who was of the bondwoman was born after the flesh,"[595] which language points to religious slavery, yet "it is the spirit that quickeneth; the flesh profiteth nothing."[596] Conversations willing to perform their belief through the smallness of their mind will deprave themselves of the intended experience. The Bible experience will only become meaningful as the mind of the conversation begins to know the living God without its religious paradigm.

13. The conversation failing to exercise its mind on the words of the Bible "is like unto a man beholding his natural face in a glass";[597] it walks away and "forgetteth what manner of man he was."[598] The conversation tied to the law of its religious tradition is, in that it exists without the directly regenerating balm of the Bible's words, a "natural" conversation. Our conversation is not to remain in this condition, but is

---

592   Philippians 3:20
593   Hebrews 12:22
594   Job 12:25
595   Galatians 4:23
596   John 6:63
597   James 1:23
598   James 1:24

to resurrect from it, which is why it is advised, "Put off concerning the former conversation the old man."[599]

14. If the conversation's goal is to keep and honor the ten precepts reflecting a diligent faith, control over that goal must be surrendered to an experience willing to have those precepts written upon the heart. As Adam was laid into the dust and formed, so too the conversation must humbly accept, for being newly created, to sleep in the dust. As our faith is laid in the dust, our error against the present learning experience will remind us of the saying, "Return unto the LORD, and he will have mercy...and to our God, for he will abundantly pardon."[600]

15. The appearance of and a performance through the conversation is, for receiving the intended edification, no longer acceptable. The defects of our personal and devotional character are to be conquered as our mind reviews, reflects on, exercises, and maintains the wisdom found within the Bible. Failing to surrender our conversation's conscience to this learning experience will disqualify our faith from the promised resurrection, even like as it says, "I will put a new spirit within you."[601]

16. Service to our conversation is not a half-hearted service. We are either for the right standard established by the Bible or we are against it. If acknowledging the living God's chief apostle as the conversation's primary example, then we must adopt that man's mind, and his mind states, "That which is born of the Spirit is spirit."[602] Thus, passing away from a stout devotion to religious law and tradition, we do well to remember how it says, "If righteousness come by the law, then Christ is dead in vain."[603]

17. "Restore unto me the joy of thy salvation,"[604] says the conversation humbling its self to confirm its belief. "Uphold me with thy free spirit,"[605] they reiterate after understanding the religious slavery

---

599   Ephesians 4:22
600   Isaiah 55:7
601   Ezekiel 11:19
602   John 3:6
603   Galatians 2:21
604   Psalms 51:12
605   Psalms 51:12

dictating their faith's experience. And how does the present wisdom within the Bible respond to these statements? It says, "If thou doest well, shalt thou not be accepted? And if thou doest not well, sin lieth at the door. And unto thee shall be his desire, and thou shalt rule over him."[606]

18. Full submission to the present philosophy within the Bible means a complete and decided removal of the heart and mind from self-developed ideas, and from cherished practices and habits, to start afresh under the substance of grace for knowledge. We do not know it, but when our faith is born within its denomination, our faith is born spiritually erroneous. The arguments given by the first apostles confirm this as fact. But this is not the end of the story. Our faith and its conversation are to resurrect from a *dead* religious experience, which is why, again, it says, "But now we are delivered from the law, that being dead wherein we were held."[607]

19. That covenant established for ancient Israel was to awaken a people dead in religious slavery to understand a living approach to spirituality. Instead of taking their *justification* through what is handwritten, these people were to see through what is handwritten to understand what is to be written without hands, even the heart of the conversation's thoughts and feelings. But they, like their contemporaries, took the act to be the end of the experience. Their condemnation is, "Laying aside the commandment of God, ye hold the tradition of men."[608]

20. The commandment of *God* was not to uphold what is handwritten; that was the charge of Moses. *God* told them, "I spake not unto your fathers, nor commanded them in the day that I brought them out of the land of Egypt, concerning burnt offerings or sacrifices. But this thing commanded I them, saying, Obey my voice."[609]

21. Is the Bible wrong? Are we reading this correctly? Are we seeing that *God*, according to the Bible, did not give the handwritten religious code? What "commandment," then, is the author of the book

---

606   Genesis 4:7
607   Romans 7:7
608   Mark 7:8
609   Jeremiah 7:22,23

of Mark referring to? Is it not that commandment stating to obey the living God's voice? What, if not through what is handwritten, is this obedience? Is the answer not found in the saying, "By his knowledge shall my righteous servant justify many"?[610]

22. "It is God which worketh in you both to will and to do of his good pleasure";[611] not what is handwritten. And again, how? It is through allowing the heart of our faith to understand the nature of the Bible's intended character, both reviewing and exercising what is learned from reviewing its pages. This is why it says, "Take no thought for your life,"[612] because when seeking to arrange, through religious law and tradition, the conversation's experience, we ruin the opportunity develop a landscape that is able to consistently edify our faith.

23. Let us say, while abstaining from religious routine and theory to remain faithful to consistently examining and exercising the Bible's counsel, "The LORD will perfect that which concerneth me."[613]

24. "Wherefore henceforth know we no man after the flesh: yea, though we have known Christ after the flesh, yet now henceforth know we him no more. Therefore if any man be in Christ he is a new creature: old things are passed away; behold, all things are become new. And all things are of God, who hath reconciled us to himself by Jesus Christ."[614]

---

610   Isaiah 53:11
611   Philippians 2:13
612   Matthew 6:25
613   Psalm 138:8
614   2 Corinthians 5:16-18

18

An Enduring Substance

1. To reject the conditions of the new covenant is to reject the healing work of grace. To reject the work of building a sane faith for maintaining a personal ideological perception of *God*, and according to preference or lifestyle, is to acknowledge the Bible, and the mind inspiring it, as an unfaithful guide. Because the intended labor of the Bible's mind is for the inward person, we do well to remember how it says, "Circumcision is that of the heart, in the spirit, and not in the letter; whose praise is not of men, but of God."[615]

2. Literal death is not the primary issue within the Bible. The death of the conversation's mind is the primary issue within the Bible, which is why it says, "Lighten mine eyes, lest I sleep the sleep of death,"[616] and, "He hath shut their eyes, that they cannot see; and their hearts,

---

615   Romans 2:29
616   Psalm 13:3

that they cannot understand."[617] The leading cause of *death* is a strict reliance on the philosophy of the religious law, or a strict reliance on a handwritten or scripted religious experience, which is why it says, "The sting of death is sin; and the strength of sin is the law."[618]

3. The present counsel is, "Circumcise the foreskin of your heart, and be no more stiffnecked."[619] What naturally covers our heart is a traditional and denominational approach and belief. This *knowledge* is what keeps our conversation prideful. And what is a prideful conversation? It is a conversation that will not personally learn the Bible's mind, even like as it says, "They did not like to retain God in their knowledge."[620]

4. But, still drawing on the analogy given by Paul, we should know that "we are not children of the bondwoman, but of the free."[621] What does this mean? It means understanding that "no man is justified by the law in the sight of God."[622] It means understanding that "through knowledge shall the just be delivered."[623] It means understanding that "we are delivered from the law,"[624] or that our conversation is to remove itself from an experience predicated upon the doing and the performing of what is handwritten to now "serve in newness of spirit."[625]

5. As the living God's chief apostle is dead, so too our conversation is to be dead with what that man's body figuratively illustrates. That minister's body, because it says, "Christ hath redeemed us from the curse of the law,"[626] figuratively represents the philosophy of the religious law. To see this body crucified and dead is to see this philosophy crucified and dead, meaning that to maintain an approach to the Bible through what is handwritten is to maintain "sin," even like as it says,

---

617   Isaiah 44:18
618   1 Corinthians 15:56
619   Deuteronomy 10:16
620   Romans 1:28
621   Galatians 4:31
622   Galatians 3:11
623   Proverbs 11:9
624   Romans 7:6
625   Romans 7:6
626   Galatians 3:13

"The strength of sin is the law."[627] If *buried* and *raised* with that man, our conversation is therefore dead to a routine by the pen of priest and minister and is raised to an experience where the mental and the inward faculties are personally discerning the living God's character.

6. It is written, "In Christ Jesus neither circumcision availeth any thing, nor uncircumcision, but a new creature. And as many as walk according to this rule, peace be on them, and mercy."[628]

7. The person is not to be literally created anew. The newness to experience is from within. The "creature" that is to surface is a conversation. Such a conversation has put off its dedication to "sin" and has accepted the Bible's present course of learning. Doing so, the conversation now has a new mind and stream of thought, even a desire to live according to the knowledge gained from intimately experiencing the Bible's words. This is why it is counseled, "Keep my commandments, and live."[629]

8. By consenting to let the present philosophy of the Bible reign over our conversation's heart and mind, our conversation will receive the intended blessing. That intended blessing is in personally knowing the Bible's character, to live by it. That intended blessing is in knowing the Bible's character so that no guide for knowing that character is needed. That intended blessing is a faith that is able to maintain itself without any outside religious source, prescription, or stimulant. That intended blessing is the fulfillment of the new covenant: "They shall teach no more every man his neighbour, and every man his brother, saying, Know the LORD: for they shall know me."[630]

9. There is now "a fountain opened to the house of David and to the inhabitants of Jerusalem for sin and for righteousness."[631] What flows from out of that fountain is the stream of an experience. That experience is one where the conversation reports, "I know him, and

---

627   1 Corinthians 15:56
628   Galatians 6:15,16
629   Proverbs 7:2
630   Jeremiah 31:34
631   Zechariah 13:1

keep his saying."[632] That experience is one where the conversation is advised, "Put off concerning the former conversation the old man, which is corrupt according to the deceitful lusts; and be renewed in the spirit of your mind."[633]

10. An experience born out of tradition will manifest itself in the disease of superstition. Because of guilt or pride, stubbornness of opinion, or the love of the religious world's character, waiting on the Bible's mind is put off, keeping the conversation from understanding fact and fiction. "This persuasion cometh not of him that calleth you."[634]

11. The present covenant, being a promise of grace for knowledge supporting the conversation's creation is, to the Bible's present mind and philosophy, the only active and recognized form of devotional approach. Our faith and its exercise, under this covenant, is what perfects the personal and devotional character. Herein time spent in a nominal profession must be exchanged for time spent learning of and proving the edifying principles of the Bible.

12. "For when we were in the flesh, the motions of sins, which were by the law, did work in our members to bring forth fruit unto death."[635] Thus, "seeing that ye have put off the old man with his deeds; and have put on the new man, which is renewed in knowledge after the image of him that created him,"[636] "being made free from sin"[637] "ye have your fruit unto holiness, and the end everlasting life."[638]

---

632   John 8:55
633   Ephesians 4:22,23
634   Galatians 5:8
635   Romans 7:5
636   Colossians 3:9,10
637   Romans 6:22
638   Romans 6:22

19

The Conversation's Task

1. What does all of this thus far discussed mean? What does it mean to let our faith suffer newness through the knowledge of the living God's character? Doubtless it means understanding the words revealing that character. So what does understanding the Bible actually mean? What of the Bible are we to understand?

2. There is a great difference between understanding the Bible's mind and understanding interpretations of the Bible's mind. Interpretations of the Bible's mind are not the Bible's mind. To understand the Bible is to dissect the philosophy of the Bible without unlawfully including self's thoughts, feelings, and notions into that examination.

3. Everyday we see interpretations of various things, even including one another, in that we interpret one another according to what we perceive. So when you see me, you will have an interpretation of me. When you see me, you may develop a number of interpretations based on my appearance, the style of my hair, what is or isn't worn on my

head, the positioning of my face and body, the color of my skin, or the sound of my voice. When you hear me, based upon the tone of my voice, the style of my dialogue, or my vocabulary, you may make more interpretations about who you think I am. But the old adage is true, (is it not?) "Don't judge a book by its cover."

4. What you see when you see me, and what you hear when you hear me, may reveal someone to you. But taking real knowledge of me, having personal dialogue and communion with me, I will not be what you thought when you actually speak to me, or when you get to know me.

5. When understanding the Bible, we are taking what we think we see, and what we think we hear, and what we think we feel, and what we think we know, and are weighing it in the balances of the Bible's intellect. What we will find is that, what we think we know and perceive of the Bible, and of the Bible's philosophy, actually doesn't exist. We don't know one thing about the Bible, or about its philosophy, but we all know *things* about the interpretations of the Bible's mind. When understanding the Bible, we are but looking for fact without self-cultivated or inherited thoughts and feelings.

6. Understanding the Bible is like understanding how a car works, or how to cook food, or how to exercise correctly. Reading interpretations of these subjects can only do so much until we actually get into the kitchen, or into the gym, or under the hood of a car, to know what is really going on.

7. And this is the key: knowing, handling, and dissecting the Bible for learning what of it to live by. The mind inspiring the Bible is as it says, "A God of knowledge."[639] This knowledge spoken of is not knowledge to obtain through books. This is a knowledge "not in the words which man's wisdom teacheth, but which the Holy Ghost teacheth."[640]

8. Knowledge is taught, but not in the way that we imagine. We have to remember that there is no physical "God" to go to. We have to understand that there is no real, tangible, or actual "God" to see

---

639 1 Samuel 2:4
640 1 Corinthians 2:13

and talk to. We have to come to grips with maintaining a faith and an experience upholding the fact that "God is a Spirit,"[641] and that "a spirit hath not flesh and bones."[642] This means that, above relying on a physical religious experience, and above relying on traditions, routines, and religious theories, our experience has to become real, even like as it says, "Through desire a man, having separated himself, seeketh and intermeddleth with all wisdom."[643]

9. We have no problem uttering and listening to the same ring of knowledge year in and year out. Our speech and comprehension of the Bible's spiritual understanding is so old, unprofitable, and obsolete that we are too scared to actually open up the Bible without an *aid*. There are no bones in what pertains to the mind; words have no flesh; remaining in what is of and for flesh and bone (a scripted religious experience) will not get the job done. If our aim is in understanding, we can't continue to rob our faith's intellect by doing what isn't in line with the Bible's course of learning.

10. We need to ask ourselves if our personal religious conversation uses prescriptions. Because if the Bible is saying to understand it, if, in relation to your idea of understanding the Bible, all you can think of are the doctrines, philosophies, and interpretations given to you by pastor so and so, and by this person and by that book or website, then you have been an abuser of religious opioids. We have been cheating our faith, and because we have been cheating our faith and its intellect, we have absolutely no idea who or what the philosophy of the Bible is, and this is a universal devotional epidemic.

11. We are sitting around, thinking that we *eat* well when, in reality, our conversation is internally, and spiritually, in poor condition. Isn't this why it says, "Wherefore do ye spend money for that which is not bread? and your labour for that which satisfieth not? hearken diligently unto me, and eat ye that which is good, and let your soul delight itself in fatness"?[644]

---

641 John 4:24
642 Luke 24:29
643 Proverbs 18:1
644 Isaiah 55:2

12. Our perception of the Bible's character needs help. We know this. But how will we approach this problem? Will we remain in what we know is not sufficient to quench our genuine need and desire for the living God? Or will we cut ties with stories and fables so that we are only left with the Bible's words? Our task, as possessing sincere conversations approaching the Bible, is in understanding how to make those words form one solid body of knowledge without misinterpretation or misunderstanding them.

13. And this isn't a difficult task. The secret to this assignment is found in the saying, "Receive my words, and hide my commandments with thee; so that thou incline thine ear unto wisdom, and apply thine heart to understanding."[645] And why should we do this? It says, "Then shalt thou understand the fear of the LORD, and find the knowledge of God."[646]

14. To understand the Bible is to understand and personally exercise the definition of the Bible's "fear." This "fear" is not like what we would think, as in anxiety, dread, concern, horror, or panic. "Fear," to the Bible's mind, as it is defined by the context in which it is used, is respectful reverence or awe for the point or fact behind the Bible's philosophy.

15. If our conversation maintains "fear," it maintains respect for the Bible's spiritual understanding. If living in "fear," our conversation is a conversation that cannot survive without the Bible's spiritual understanding. If living in "fear," our faith does not carry a religious conversation founded upon public or private opinion or interpretation, but our faith maintains its self by the knowledge we retain or acquire when learning of and doing the Bible's words. This is why it says, "Be ye transformed by the renewing of your mind, that ye may prove what is that good, and acceptable, and perfect, will of God."[647]

16. There is a difference in executing the Bible's words and doing what we think those words are saying. Our goal, so that we may benefit from it both personally and devotionally, should be to comprehend what

---

645   Proverbs 2:1,2
646   Proverbs 2:5
647   Romans 12:2

the Bible is saying for increasing "fear." This means that we have to risk something very dear and important to us if desiring to successfully complete this assignment, and that risk comes in the form of suffering the loss of our natural spiritual landscape. This should be no surprise, especially when it says, "I count all things but loss for the excellency of the knowledge of Christ."[648]

---

648   Philippians 3:8

20

Loss

1. Our conversation needs the Bible's "fear," and if it says, "The fear of the LORD is the beginning of knowledge,"[649] then what we need, in reality, is knowledge of the Bible's will and wisdom.

2. The Bible tells us the type of devotional character it cannot stand, saying, "They hated knowledge, and did not choose the fear of the LORD,"[650] and, "As they did not like to retain God in their knowledge, God gave them over to a reprobate mind."[651] It is even anciently said, "I desired mercy, and not sacrifice, and the knowledge of God more than burnt offerings."[652]

3. These verses prove the principle established in the previous chapter, that a confidence built up by interpretation, and not by

---

649 Proverbs 1:7
650 Proverbs 1:29
651 Romans 1:28
652 Hosea 6:6

knowledge personally acquired, is a false manner to maintain our personal faith by. There is a more sure way to maintain the character and the experience of our faith, and while the answer is according to the saying, "Through knowledge shall the just be delivered,"[653] the means whereby the answer is understood is "loss."

4. The mind within the Bible, from the verses just mentioned in the books of Proverbs and Hosea, understands that we can carry our conversation in two ways: the first way is through various sacrifices, offerings, commandments, and baptisms; the second way is through exercising "fear" for knowledge. The Bible knows the value of knowledge to our experience, which is why it says, "My people are destroyed for lack of knowledge,"[654] and, "Fools die for want of wisdom."[655]

5. The key to understanding the Bible is our experience with the Bible. Our faith needs to personally experience just what the living God's will is if it will ever "fear" or respect it. Our faith needs the experience of learning how to know just what in it is to be resurrected, reformed, and edified. Our faith needs, according to the Bible, a real and living experience with its words, and not an experience in what is considered to be a *sacrifice* or an *offering*.

6. Our main concern should be the Bible's "fear," and if the Bible itself is saying this, we should listen. We should listen because if "fear" is through knowledge, and if knowledge is through personally experiencing the Bible's wisdom, then if we have never experienced any *thing* within the Bible, we have never really experienced the Bible. We may have experienced our perception of *God*. We may be experiencing what religious tradition tells us to experience of *God*. But if we are not genuinely experiencing the Bible's will and wisdom for knowledge to live by, we have, and are, experiencing nothing.

7. Isn't it great to do and to have full knowledge of an activity? Isn't it great to do and to never have to guess at what is being done? We are doing and do not have to pause to think about what we are doing because we are, both mentally and emotionally, engaged. When

---

653 Proverbs 11:9
654 Hosea 4:6
655 Proverbs 10:21

we take knowledge of something, we are mentally and emotionally engaged. It is our engagement, for always enjoying that particular thing we are doing, that allows us to retain memory of what we are learning.

8. Emotion plays a major role in learning; this is why it says, "By the sadness of the countenance the heart is made better. The heart of the wise is in the house of mourning."[656] What we feel dictates what we care to learn. Sorrow is here portrayed as a positive instrument for learning because a genuinely sorrowful heart possesses a humble spirit, and humility attracts wisdom, even like as it says, "With the lowly is wisdom."[657]

9. To understand the Bible means to allow the heart to feel the character within the Bible. To feel the character within the Bible means to mentally and emotionally engage with it. This engagement will enlighten the perception, giving to the understanding a "fear" forwarding exercise for wisdom. It is this exercise, because one is retaining knowledge of the Bible's character, and because that knowledge is revealing an incorrect service to that character, that will inspire the conversation to correct its self, even like as it says, "Godly sorrow worketh repentance to salvation."[658]

10. This is how we are to let our faith understand the Bible. There's no such thing as having someone drink water for you, and then you feeling as though you aren't thirsty anymore. This is the problem with ingesting interpretations on the Bible's mind; they always leave us *thirsty*. This is why we are counseled, "Seek ye out of the book of the LORD, and read."[659]

11. The Bible is plain. The Bible is against our heaping together and feasting on interpretations of its mind. So it appears that we have to make a decision: will we suffer the loss of what we consider to be true *knowledge* for a real experience with the Bible, or not? Is our faith, in order to receive knowledge to live and operate by, willing to suffer the kind of loss it needs?

---

656   Ecclesiastes 7:3,4
657   Proverbs 11:2
658   2 Corinthians 7:10
659   Isaiah 34:16

12. To claim or achieve the understanding we desire within the Bible, a certain personal loss is needed. This loss is necessary for right knowledge on the Bible's science, which loss is according to the saying, "I count all things but loss for the excellency of the knowledge of Christ."[660]

13. A key part of understanding the Bible's language is always remembering that this book is firstly a book of philosophy, and should be applied firstly as a book of philosophy. Hearing Paul say, "I gave up all things and do but count all things but loss," does not and should not move us to read what he is saying in a literal or secular sense. The context in which he is speaking is in relation to knowledge. The "things" that Paul has given up are "things" related to his philosophical and spiritual understanding of the scriptures, even like as he says, "Not having mine own righteousness, which is of the law."[661]

14. The spiritual mind is to regulate and counsel the corporeal or natural mind. The physical or natural mind is not to govern and counsel its mind plus the devotional mind. We will lose our mind if the natural mind governs the complete essence, both inward and physical, of our *being*, moving us to become one possessing the statement, "The good that I would I do not: but the evil which I would not, that I do."[662]

15. The *things* that Paul suffered the loss of were, in right context of language, religious *things*, and we know this by how he blatantly states his desire to relinquish claiming *righteousness* through religious laws and policies. Paul was willing to suffer the loss of a *righteousness* given through handwritten religious tradition because it negatively impacts the person, giving them pride through a false and sensual confidence, even like as it says, "Which things have indeed a shew of wisdom in will worship,"[663] and, "All their works they do for to be seen of men."[664]

16. The foundational principle that the first apostles taught was the renewal or the resurrection of the spiritual understanding without

---

660   Philippians 3:8
661   Philippians 3:9
662   Romans 7:19
663   Colossians 2:23
664   Matthew 23:5

relying upon inherited or adopted religious tradition. We understand that this was a philosophical position of theirs from how it says, for example, "Know that ye were not redeemed with corruptible things, as silver and gold, from your vain conversation received by tradition,"[665] and, "Put off concerning the former conversation the old man...and be renewed in the spirit of your mind."[666]

17. Our willingness to suffer the loss of our darling religious theories and beliefs is the key unlocking our sure relationship with the Bible's will and wisdom. But of course, there must first be a desire for the Bible's will and wisdom, and for every conversation possessing such a desire, it says, "Through desire a man, having separated himself, seeketh and intermeddleth with all wisdom."[667]

18. The Bible is advising our conversation to make a much-needed change in how it approaches it. We need to change how we think and feel on the Bible, and that means patiently and temperately understanding how to let our faith learn how to live. Such an assignment calls for a change in our spiritual, mental, or philosophical diet, and the mind within the Bible, if our desire is to know its character, counsels us to do so.

19. In order to gain the faith we want, we have to be willing to lose the faith we have. This is why it says, "He that loveth his life shall lose it; and he that hateth his life in this world shall keep it unto life eternal."[668] And we need not fear, seeing as how this exercise is for allowing our conversation to know that the Creator is in the business of restoring and resurrecting. This is why it says, "Create in me a clean heart, O God; and renew a right spirit within me."[669]

---

665   1 Peter 1:18
666   Ephesians 4:22,23
667   Proverbs 18:1
668   John 12:25
669   Psalm 51:12

21

The Allegory

1. The Bible makes a rather interesting point when saying that, in order to gain, or rather to regain a sure and intelligent faith, we have to lose our former devotional confidence. This is, despite the prevailing philosophy within the Bible of *sanctity* or *favor* through doing or performing handwritten religious laws, the present and underlying philosophy within the Bible. If we cannot understand this key narrative within the scriptures, we will not possess the faith intended by the Bible, and will never know that "the law is not of faith."[670]

2. The Bible's "fear," because its knowledge possesses a ministry for creation, is philosophy grounded in creation. The ultimate goal behind the Bible's science is creation, and if we would have our conversation become a creation of the Bible's mind, we have to put away or

---

670   Galatians 3:12

refrain from what stops, prevents, or halts the type of creation the Bible promotes.

3. We should know if we do or do not want our conversation to be a creation of the Bible's will and wisdom. The living God inspiring the Bible's will and wisdom has only one office, and that office is for creating, and if we have an issue with passing through creation's process, what the mind within the Bible has to offer us will be of no value.

4. The concern within the Bible is not a natural concern for our conversation. Hear the Bible's concern: "Whosoever will save his life shall lose it: and whosoever will lose his life for my sake shall find it."[671]

5. Is the Bible literally encouraging us to kill ourselves? Does the Bible want its reader to literally sacrifice their life for it? The language is allegorical, and being figurative, it is pointing to the fact that the *life* or the confidence of our conversation must, for the sake of receiving the intended creation, be sacrificed.

6. Is this hard to think about? Is this a saying that should make us say, "This is an hard saying; who can hear it?"[672] If it is, it is only difficult to rationalize because we are unnaturally tied to some religious "thing" that we must let go of. The Bible is calling for us to commit suicide but, in right context, the "us" isn't personal or actual. The "us" that must be killed is not our natural self, but our religious self.

7. Remember, as stated in the last chapter, the Bible is firstly a book whose context is philosophical. If we will not patiently and temperately abstain from what we think a Bible experience is, we will never come to know what that experience is. We are advised to kill our traditional understanding so that we can gain a real and living understanding of what is demanded for our conversation and its conscience.

8. Again, what must be annihilated is our "life," and this "life" is not our natural "life," but rather our religious "life." We have to know that "there is a natural body, and there is a spiritual body."[673]

9. The nature or context of the living God is not natural, like ours. We actually receive knowledge of the living God's nature from how it

---

671   Matthew 16:25
672   John 6:60
673   1 Corinthians 15:44

says, "God is a Spirit."[674] And so, when it comes to our conversation's growth and development, we have to think rationally, and very carefully, because if it will say, "A spirit hath not flesh and bones,"[675] and *God* is yet a spirit and not flesh and bones, there must be, above a flesh-based reliance on what stimulates and settles our natural mind, a better way to enter into the Bible's intended learning experience.

10. If it says, "A spirit hath not flesh and bones,"[676] if we are saying that the living God is a Creator without flesh and bones, we must not disassociate the form of the Creator from the form of his creation. If we will accept what the Bible is saying, and we do well to accept what it is saying, that *God* is a *Spirit*, if looking or seeking to be created by "God," we cannot envision the manifestation of that creation as being physical, or as initially occurring in a realm that is natural. This is why it says, "That which is born of the Spirit is spirit."[677]

11. Think of it like this: does an automobile mechanic fix automobiles or airplanes? A car mechanic, beings familiar with the internal and the external parts of the automobile, is a car mechanic, and an airplane mechanic, being familiar with the internal and the external parts of an airplane, is an airplane mechanic. The car mechanic works with what his preferred object is, and when it comes to cars, because his mind is trained for and geared towards cars, he repairs only cars.

12. The living God is a mechanic for the heart and mind of our conversation's conscience. The Bible's service is firstly useless to the natural body but firstly beneficial for the *body* of our faith. If the living God were like us, being actually and consistently physically, then we may say that the Bible's service is firstly physical, being obtained through a natural or flesh-based form of devotion. But being *Spirit*, the living God's number one concern is for that "body" similar to its own, which is why the living God's chief apostle taught, concerning this matter of creation, "That which is born of the Spirit is spirit."[678]

---

674   John 4:24
675   Luke 24:39
676   Luke 24:29
677   John 3:6
678   John 3:6

13. Creation, as we saw from the previous chapter, is to occur inwardly. Because creation occurs inwardly, the intended creation is for the spirit of our faith's mind, and we know this because Paul, when speaking on the subject of creation, tell us that our conversation's mind is "to be strengthened with might by his Spirit in the inner man."[679] The inward person of our conversation is to presently experience creation, and this creation, as Paul says, is through "strength," and if through "strength," we need to know how the Bible defines "strength."

14. We find the definition of "strength," or of what "strengthens," in the book of Ecclesiastes chapter seven and verse nineteen. It says, "Wisdom strengtheneth." Strength and wisdom are interchangeable terms, even like as it says, "With him is strength and wisdom, he hath counsel and understanding,"[680] and, "He is mighty in strength and wisdom."[681]

15. We now have a very important Bible principle: in order to benefit from the Bible's "fear," or from its spiritual understanding, our faith needs to be strengthened by the wisdom, understanding, or counsel within it, and by no *thing* else. Whatever is stopping this wisdom from reaching us, we need to lose or abandon it, because when this wisdom is within our faith's mind, it will change how we think and feel about who we are, and about our external world.[682]

16. Our goal is to consciously and consistently benefit from the Bible's wisdom. As opposed to a mindless service behind religious tradition, or through what appears to be agreeable through sensually stimulating our thoughts, feelings, actions, and behavior, the initial apostles' doctrine focused on faith's personal cultivation.

17. The foundation of their doctrine comes from examining the allegory behind the illustration of the living God's man suffering the tree, or the cross. To them, this illustration presented the revelation of an allegory explaining the present reality of the living God's will and wisdom. Paul helps us to understand just what all of this means in

---

679   Ephesians 3:16
680   Job 12:13
681   Job 36:5
682   Proverbs 2:10,11

one phrase: "Having abolished in his flesh the enmity, even the law of commandments contained in ordinances."[683]

18. According to the philosophy that Paul is giving, when it comes to that man's body on the tree, or on the cross, we should not look at it as the body of a human male. That body represents something, and according to what Paul is saying, that body represents a religious philosophy. This religious philosophy is a doctrine stating human and religious *righteousness, pardon, piety, favor, forgiveness, beauty*, and *intellect*, by handwritten religious laws.

19. As the initial apostles studied the vision of the living God's man suffering the tree, they all equally learned that the philosophy nailed to the tree is harmful to the person and their faith, teaching, "The strength of sin is the law."[684] It was through investigating what the man's crucifixion figuratively represented that they learned the mystery behind *creation's* present science, that "Christ hath redeemed us from the curse of the law."[685]

20. The science behind the illustration of the living God's man suffering crucifixion is the "fear" we should presently have for the living God. The illustration of this man suffering the tree is an illustration depicting what our personal religious conversation should suffer, which is a loss of self-righteous religious behaviors and beliefs for a conversation that is resurrected, thoughtful, and sound.

---

683   Ephesians 2:15
684   1 Corinthians 15:56
685   Galatians 3:13

22

In Right Light

1. When hearing that it says, "He that loveth his life shall lose it; and he that hateth his life in this world shall keep it unto life eternal,"[686] it is not hard to see that what the Bible values is different from what our conversation naturally values. Our conversation wants to control its *life*. Our conversation believes that it owns its *life*. For some reason, our conversation forgets that "every good gift and every perfect gift is from above."[687] To us, giving our faith to an experience with the Bible's words makes absolutely no sense, but to the Bible, our faith doesn't exist without personally knowing its words.

2. Should we look closer at what actually took place on the tree, or on the cross, we will find that one "life" was sacrificed for another "life." The illustration of the living God's chief apostle suffering the

---

686 John 12:25
687 James 1:17

tree teaches an exchange of conversations figuratively occurring, which occurrence is an important revelation for our faith to discern.

3. On the tree, or on the cross, there are two "lives" within one man. When we hear, "When Jesus had cried with a loud voice, he said, Father, into thy hands I commend my spirit: and having said thus, he gave up the ghost,"[688] we are hearing that one "life" passed away from existence, but that another "life," being kept by the living God, is given the power and privilege to replace that formerly sacrificed and relinquished "life." In this act we see the Bible's present concern. This concern is for the regeneration of some *thing*, and for the reformation of some *thing*.

4. The author of the book of John writes that whosoever hates their "life" in this "world" will not only keep it, but will keep it for ever, meaning that it will never decay, decline, or pass away. Because we learn of two lives, or conversations, existing within the living God's chief apostle, and that when on the tree, the act of extinguishing one "life" for another "life" occurs, we may know that there is a "life" born for annihilation, or born to pass away, and that there is a "life" that is born to never pass away. Our assignment, and our desire, should be to possess that "life" the living God magnifies, hating that "life" within the "world" to claim it.

5. Briefly, before moving on, in order to bring greater clarity to the message within this chapter, it is well to understand the context of the word "world." The Bible is primarily a book of philosophy or analogy, and in its first context, the words of the Bible are to be applied not secularly, but spiritually or philosophically. Herein we may know the "world" spoken of is not a reference to the natural world, but to the religious world, even like as it says, "I spake openly to the world; I ever taught in the synagogue, and in the temple, wither the Jews always resort."[689]

6. The "world" in reference is the world of religion, or the religious world, and more specifically, the *world* of the religion of the *Jews*. The

---

688   Luke 23:46
689   John 18:20

"life" that we are to hate is that life intimately connected with that philosophy forwarding the Jews' religion.

7. Our conversation, when it is conceived, is conceived in "sin." What does this mean? Think about how you know what you know on the *Bible's* experience, and how you carry out that experience. Think about this in terms of understanding where it came from. How do you know *God*? How are you hearing about how to carry your faith? Where do your ideas about how to carry your faith come from? What does your general religious philosophy of a perfect faith come from, and by what means is it achieved? The answers to all of these questions are that what is known is also regulated by some thought founded upon some notion conveyed by some religious law or theory.

8. The religious world operates through the philosophy of "sin." When our conversation is conceived within the religious world, it is a conversation that is naturally "sinful," or it is a conversation that is naturally negligent towards the character of the living God's will and wisdom. This is why we cannot forget this concept of two "lives" preached by the Bible. There is one "life" that, as it says in the book of John, is of the "world," and another that is without the "world," even like as it says, "Our conversation is in heaven."[690] Our responsibility is to hate that *life* or conversation of the "world," which "life" is natural to us. We are to therefore love and edify our "life" without the *world*, which "life" is not natural us, but is experienced and given as it is cultivated.

9. The "world" that is referenced is not the natural or secular world. A living experience with the Bible isn't about quitting or hiding from the secular or the natural world, because if it were, how would we ever have the opportunity to be a blessing to inquiring minds? A living experience with the Bible doesn't put the person away from the natural world, but from the religious world, from the heart and philosophical confidence within the religious world. And we can safely say this due to how it says, "Pure religion and undefiled before God and the Father

---

690   Philippians 3:20

is this, To visit the fatherless and widows in their affliction, and to keep himself unspotted from the world."[691]

10. If it is important to know the Mind inspiring the Bible, if we will understand the Bible, if our goal is to know the Bible's devotional character, then the Bible is what we need to know and not an interpretation of the Bible's mind from within the religious world. What we know or understand of the Bible comes from the religious world's *circle* and not from the Bible. Thus, to say plainly, within this crucified *body* rests two conversations supporting two different religious philosophies: the first conversation and philosophy is based upon the religious code of the religious world; the second conversation and philosophy is based upon the Bible's wisdom of creation. What we are seeing, when observing this man crucified, is the death and separation of one religious conversation from the Bible's devotional character and the blessing of another. This other conversation rightly justifies the underlying devotional character within the scriptures.

11. What was killed was that "life" of the religious world, but what ascended heavenward was that "life" of the Bible's spiritual understanding. This act is a lesson or parable to help us understand what is true and false religion. And Paul, to help us better understand what false religion is, writes, when talking about that killed "life," "Having abolished in his flesh the enmity, even the law of commandments contained in ordinances."[692]

12. The body of that man nailed to the tree represents the philosophy of the religious world. This philosophy, as we have already discussed, is a religion where handwritten religious laws and traditions justify the person before *God*. This is a false religion because the illustration of the crucifixion blatantly teaches that "Christ hath redeemed us from the curse of the law, being made a curse for us: for it is written, Cursed is every one that hangeth on a tree."[693]

13. The lesson is that we, for the growth and maturity of our faith, are to hate what the living God hates. The Bible's devotional character

---

691   James 1:27
692   Ephesians 2:15
693   Galatians 3:13

presently dislikes, because this is not the definition of true religion, the inventing and the employing of religious laws and traditions used to define the conversation. True religion is, according to what is taught by this man suffering crucifixion, without handwritten religious laws and traditions, and we may confidently say so due to how it says justification and salvation is not "through the law, but through the righteousness of faith."[694]

14. We need to ask ourselves if we today hate what is advised to be hated and love what is advised. Think about what you are serving, and how, because a lying and a deceiving *Jesus*, forwarding an abolished religious approach, is at work. This *figure* tells our conversation that it is right for our faith to suffer the doctrinal code of the religious world, but from what is taught by the Bible, it is unhealthy to digest the findings of the *world's scientist*. We understand the Bible's position from how it says, "He that loveth his life shall lose it; and he that hateth his life in this world shall keep it unto life eternal."[695]

15. We have to lose our spiritual confidence in order to actually possess it, and this is the point. We wouldn't allow someone to put a literal leash on our neck, directing our steps by their steps. So our Creator is asking, "Why do you allow a spiritual chain around your neck?" The Bible wants us to question, "Why is my liberty judged of another man's conscience?"[696]

16. We can't understand the Bible when our conversation is tied to another religious philosophy. When we let go of the religious world's spiritual perception, then, and only then, will we clearly perceive the character of the Bible's will and wisdom in its right light.

---

694   Romans 4:13
695   John 12:25
696   1 Corinthians 10:29

23

For Our Confidence

1. To claim a faith that is credible, and that can claim the intended creation, we are to hate our conversation that is born through the practices and principles of the religious world. These practices and principles are in justifying or establishing the devotional conversation through doing and believing on handwritten religious laws and traditions. And it may seem as though this is an attack on the religion of Moses. It is not. This is why it says, "Whatsoever God doeth, it shall be for ever: nothing can be put to it, nor any thing taken from it: and God doeth it, that men should fear before him."[697]

2. What took place through the tree is an eternal event. No matter what age of life we are in, no matter what generation of life walks this earth, Moses' religious philosophy is categorized as "sin." Any *Moses*, since the living God's man suffered the tree, preaching *divine*

----

697   Ecclesiastes 3:14

134

favor, justification, or *righteousness* by the religious law is against the Bible's will and wisdom. Again, it is not that the religious philosophy of the Moses of that ancient age is singled out and destroyed through the crucifixion, but that in every age after this event, without end, any resemblance to the religious philosophy of Moses is to be observed as "sin," even like as it says, "Not only in this world, but also in that which is to come,"[698] and, "The strength of sin is the law."[699]

3. What is figuratively preached through the crucifixion actually reveals a benevolent agenda for the human and their devotional character. If you think about it, we all possess individual governments within our human being. In history, do we ever find one nation content with being subjected under another nation? When one nation finds themselves unwillingly subject to another nation, sure they may suffer for a time, but eventually they rise up to defend themselves against their oppressor. Even prophecy reveals the oppression of a *people* honoring the Bible's full wisdom and experience, but at the end of the controversy it says, "They shall take them captives, whose captives they were; and they shall rule over their oppressors."[700]

4. To understand the Bible is to understand the law of liberty that it preaches. Just like one nation of people will not forever accept the oppression of another, but will, although at first unable to do anything about it, rise up to eventually fight for their liberty, so we cannot any longer, through inherited or self-cultivated slavery to the religious world's spiritual mind, let the *government* of our personal faith suffer under that *body* we have.

5. Do you think you could, if asked, explain what the worst form of slavery is? It is the kind of slavery made to appear as though it is not slavery. The worst kind of slavery is a fashionable oppression, an oppression making you think you excel when, in reality, you are only walking in a circle.

6. The revelation of the living God's chief minister suffering the tree is the revelation of a law of liberty. This is a liberty from putting

---

698   Ephesians 1:21
699   1 Corinthians 15:56
700   Isaiah 14:2

faith in malnourishing spiritual opinions and routines to say, "Why is my liberty judged of another man's conscience?"[701] and, "I know him, and keep his saying."[702]

7. The conversation's consciousness is the living God's goal. To understand the Bible is to understand its will or intention, which will is, as Paul says, to "purge your conscience from dead works to serve the living God."[703]

8. Consciousness to our conversation's conscience is the Bible's ultimate position, and we can only say so by what is preached through that man suffering the tree. Because "sin" takes our faith away from reality, adding consciousness to our faith's mind involves us being able to comprehend the present definition of "sin." We may today, by carefully observing what is taught through the illustration of that man suffering the tree, know the definition of "sin," that "the strength of sin is the law."[704]

9. Because, being conceived through the *womb* of the religious world, our conversation has no pure understanding of the Bible's devotional character, we do not know what "sin" is. "Sin" is not firstly secular, or firstly natural or physical, but if we are seeking to define "sin" according to how the Bible defines "sin," then "sin" must firstly be understood as being drawn from a context that is religious or philosophical.

10. The Bible must be understood according to the context that it provides. We can read whatever we may read within the Bible, and we may interpret whatever we may interpret from whatever we read, but if our interpretation escapes the context of the Bible, then we interpret through a faulty lens.

11. The Bible is a book correcting religious philosophy. It makes no sense, if seeking wisdom or understanding through the Bible, to firstly utter a physical or flesh-based judgment from what is ultimately devotional counsel. To take what is primarily for religion as

---

701   1 Corinthians 10:29
702   John 8:55
703   Hebrews 9:14
704   1 Corinthians 15:56

firstly given to the natural life is a wrong against the words and spirit establishing the Bible's context.

12. When hearing about "sin," the first concern of "sin" is not against self, but is against the living God's counsel. Self suffers abuse, or we willingly suffer abuse upon ourselves, because we fail to know how to properly understand and apply the Bible's instruction. If we commit error against the Bible, we shouldn't think that whatever wrong occurs in the natural body is firstly a wrong against *God*, because we aren't *God*, and *God* isn't living this natural life for us. Wrongs against the body are done against self; violence against you is against you; no matter what you do to you, the living God remains as is. But a simple definition of "sin" is doing what stops the devotional conversation from actively and honestly knowing and participating in the Creator's will and wisdom.

13. The Creator's chief apostle defines "sin" through the tree, that "sin" is suffering the handwritten religious law on the conversation's conscience. We can't forget that the controversy witnessed at the crucifixion is between two religious philosophies: one would have the mind enslaved by a routine religious service; the other would have the mind liberated from a routine religious service to faithfully honor the words and the experience of the present science of *creation*.

14. The philosophy preached through the illustration of this man suffering the tree is important because it shows how the living God sees the manner in which we ought to carry our faith. Religion shouldn't swallow up who we are, like as how water swallows up our body when we are entered into the ocean, or in a pool. Religion should cause those waters to part or divide as we walk, preparing a clear ground for us to travel to the destination of the person we are meant to be. And this is the point. We are all born to fulfill a mission in this life, but the more our mind is chained to and by invented religious philosophy, the more we fail to actually realize just what the living God's will is for us.

15. When understanding the Bible, we understand the wisdom that is given for us to reach our highest human and devotional potential, and to reach our highest potential not even for our own self, but for the conscience of other conversations. This is what makes the

development of our faith so important. Our confidence should not remain on what we think we know, or on the religious information we inherit, but should be founded upon an experience adding wisdom not only to who we are, but also to who we are created to be.

24

Conception's Draw

1. There is no greater good for the soul than witnessing another rightly comprehending *creation's* present will and wisdom. The impression made upon the mind when "rightly dividing the word of truth"[705] is an experience that every conversation must know. There is no thing better than experiencing the refreshing within the Bible's philosophy to "be filled with the knowledge of his will in all wisdom and spiritual understanding,"[706] only to continue examining the scriptures for creating maps of understanding to more efficiently discern its voice, even like as it says, "That your love may abound yet more and more in knowledge and in all judgment."[707]

2. If our understanding on heavenly *things* is not increasing, neither is our joy in heavenly *things* increasing. Our private sessions

---

705   2 Timothy 2:15
706   Colossians 1:9
707   Philippians 1:9,10

with the Bible are to help keep our mind on what is "excellent," even as it says, "His name alone is excellent,"[708] and, "Praise him according to his excellent greatness."[709] Without personally examining the *name* of the Creator's greatness; which name is "the kindness and love of God our Saviour toward man";[710] our understanding will never receive right nourishment to keep and to govern the body of our faith, but if we are learning of and doing the judgment of that *name*, then we are entered in to its manner of baptism to love that *name*, self, and other minds. The love offered to self through the wisdom acquired is only half of the joy of this communion. Our joy is made full when the same mind and experience edifying our conversation edifies another mind.

3. Edification is the Bible's intention, and this refreshing cannot commence if not through learning of, examining, and doing its will and wisdom, even as it says, "I will meditate in thy precepts, and have respect unto thy ways."[711] Because "that which is born of the Spirit is spirit,"[712] the blessing of creation sits only upon the spirit of the mind, which is why we are counseled, "Be renewed in the spirit of your mind."[713] If we are failing to mentally review and spiritually discern the Bible's words, we will fail to obtain a clear understanding of the living God's *voice* to possess a confident assurance of its promise.

4. Right love begins when the person cares for their own self, which is why we are told, "Every one that asketh receiveth; and he that seeketh findeth; and to him that knocketh it shall be opened."[714] When there is enough concern for self that the person seeks for blessing to receive and keep blessing, that person will know the goodness of the living God's *name*. Because this blessing is through the Bible's present wisdom, the conversation inquires within the book holding salvation's context, and by consistent and diligent examination, is opened up to

---

708   Psalm 148:13
709   Psalm 150:2
710   Titus 3:4
711   Psalm 119:15
712   John 3:6
713   Ephesians 4:23
714   Luke 11:10

the revelation of their heart to learn sobriety for their person, even as it says, "A sound heart is the life of the flesh."[715]

5. Acquiring soundness by personally examining and doing *creation's* will; as it says, "In his law doth he meditate day and night";[716] is the beginning of godly charity to self, and that benevolence is forwarded when assisting another mind on their journey to know the living God. This is an experience that none should miss or put off, and we understand this fact from how it says of E'noch, "E'noch lived sixty and five years, and begat Methu'selah: and E'noch walked with God after he begat Methu'selah three hundred years, and begat sons and daughters."[717]

6. E'noch's conversation, before he conceived a son, was as every other. E'noch lived sixty-five years in stillness, but then, after the birth of his son, it not only records that he walked with *God*, but that he was taken of *God* from among *men*. This record allows us to understand that, as powerful as our conversion is when under the wings of the philosophy taught by the Bible, there is no other thing comparable to the birth of a child.

7. E'noch's son was not his literal child, even as it was told to Abraham, "He that shall come forth out of thine own bowels shall be thine heir."[718] The "bowels" of the person is the heart of the person, even as it says, "My bowels are troubled; mine heart is turned within me,"[719] and, "My heart is like wax; it is melted in the midst of my bowels."[720] Methu'selah is a product of E'noch's "bowels," becoming a "son" by the doctrine given to E'noch through the *words* that he taught.

8. Methu'selah, in right context, is a "son" according to how it says, "Mine own son after the common faith,"[721] and, "As a son with

---

715   Proverbs 13:40a
716   Psalm 1:2
717   Genesis 5:21,22
718   Genesis 15:4
719   Lamentations 1:20
720   Psalm 22:14
721   Titus 1:4

the father, he hath served with me in the gospel."[722] This "son" of E'noch is a minister of E'noch's spiritual understanding, and E'noch, for sixty-five years, maintained his conversation without a son, but after a son was born through his own *bowels*, his entire world changed, so much so that his *name* and *confidence* ceased to exist among men and was found within the *heavenly* Sanctuary.

9. The conception of a chief steward meant a lot to E'noch, for it confirmed to him the doctrine of his *LORD*. There is no name mentioned by Adam's book of generations confessing a right walk with creation's *God* other than E'noch. Sons and daughters proceed from every name on that list, and chief sons of their fathers are mentioned, but there is no experience recorded within that book of generations as telling as E'noch's.

10. After Methu'selah, E'noch's understanding was directed to the *LORD's* intention among *men*. His conversation transformed through Methu'selah, for it is evident that he wanted a *son*, but the manner in which he went about it, and for sixty-five years, may have been a wrong approach. And it is not as though he did not uphold a faithful conversation, because he did, but after Methu'selah came about, his conversation became perfect, for he now heard the saying, "Walk before me, and be thou perfect."[723] If there is then no mentioning of his walk before Methu'selah, it is that his walk was not as perfect as it could have been, and "perfect, as pertaining to the conscience."[724] After Methu'selah, E'noch perfected his conversation within his conscience, which is why it is no surprise that "he was not,"[725] for his conversation resurrected.

11. It is well to remember that "God," from Genesis to the Revelation, is the living God's "word" or "wisdom"; "in the beginning was the Word, and the Word was with God, and the Word was God."[726]

---

722 Philippians 2:22
723 Genesis 17:1
724 Hebrews 9:9
725 Genesis 5:24
726 John 1:1

When hearing, concerning E'noch, that "God took him,"[727] we are hearing that wisdom took E'noch. Now, "the Word of life"[728] is "the Spirit of life";[729] the Bible's *Word* is the Bible's *Spirit*. Because "that which is born of the Spirit is spirit,"[730] this *Wisdom* or *Word*, when it comes to E'noch, fulfills the saying, "These were redeemed from among men."[731] This record in Genesis allows us to understand the age in which E'noch lived, because, if the wisdom of the living God took him, then the age belonged to the wisdom of *men*.

12. If, according to the Bible, a perfect conversation maintains its self through its mind; as it says, "Live according to God in the spirit";[732] then it is that an imperfect conversation is one failing to operate through the spirit of the mind, executing what "sanctifieth to the purifying of the flesh,"[733] being a conversation that does "glory in appearance, and not in heart."[734] To glory in heart is to edify the inward parts, but to glory in appearance is to *bless* the show of a religious conversation by deeds, doctrines, and acts. An imperfect conversation establishes unrighteousness, and "all unrighteousness is sin,"[735] "and the strength of sin is the law."[736]

13. The conversation, through the spirit of its mind, is to exist without religious laws and traditions for knowledge on how to keep its self, but by the religious law of *men*, or of theologians, the conversation exists without its mind, relying on a routine for *blessing*. E'noch, not being found among *men*, is a confession that he correctly honored the Bible's intended philosophy. In his age, "the enmity, even the law of commandments contained in ordinances"[737] ruled among ministers and elders, but E'noch quit their shadow to stand under the living

---

727 Genesis 5:24
728 1 John 1:1
729 Revelation 11:11
730 John 3:6
731 Revelation 14:4
732 1 Peter 4:6
733 Hebrews 9:13
734 2 Corinthians 5:12
735 1 John 5:17
736 1 Corinthians 15:56
737 Ephesians 2:15

God's wisdom. E'noch is so recognized because he, above every minister in his age, consecrated his conversation to law of *creation*, and so much so that his conversation vanished away from the religious world and took on a new *form*.

14. Herein we may understand how Noah "became heir of the righteousness which is by faith."[738] Noah learned *creation's* lost doctrine by an experimental faith on the living God's *voice* through *E'noch*, which is why it is no surprise that it says of Noah, "Noah was a just man and perfect in his generations, and Noah walked with God."[739] E'noch was the first to wholeheartedly do this and Noah came after him. Like Noah, who being taken by the same wisdom remained on *earth* and ministered, the same lot fell to E'noch, who dwelt in the living God's *mountain* preaching, "We are the circumcision, which worship God in the spirit."[740]

15. E'noch's understanding would never have become so mighty if it was not for Methu'selah's conception. E'noch did have a love for his *LORD* before Methu'selah, but he never sincerely confessed to a "love in the Spirit."[741] Caught up with his age, as just as he was, E'noch was similar in word and in deed as the other *men* in his age, who operated through that "sin" made famous by Eve. But then after sixty-five years of praying for a son, E'noch's demeanor changed, and by the impression made upon Methu'selah, he lifted up his *eyes* heavenward and never brought them back down to the *earth*. E'noch, before Methu'selah's conception, professed a conversation by "a shew of wisdom in will worship,"[742] but after Methu'selah, this man possessed a perfect conversation with the living God's will.

16. E'noch's record is proof that the experience of witnessing a mind rightly discerning heaven's operation is that knowledge perfecting joy in the personal religion, which is why we are counseled, "And above all these things put on charity, which is the bond

---

738   Hebrews 11:7
739   Genesis 6:9
740   Philippians 3:3
741   Colossians 1:8
742   Colossians 2:23

of perfectness."[743] Herein, through E'noch, we may understand that an unmolested confidence before the Bible's Wisdom or Word determines a perfect conversation, but what seals that perfect faith is self-sacrificing charity.

---

743   Colossians 3:14

25

Kindness To Live By

1. It is the responsibility of every conversation not only impressed by the living God's wisdom, but also resurrected and reformed by this commandment, to refresh other minds. The living God has not opened up the doors of *salvation's heavenly* Sanctuary for only a select few to enter, but by that course of learning offered through the mediation of that Building's wisdom, all are to be gathered together, even as it says, "In the place where it was said unto them, Ye are not my people, there it shall be said unto them, Ye are the sons of the living God."[744]

2. It is the responsibility of the conversation personally trained in the will of the Bible's wisdom to care for the heritage of that philosophy. Knowledge is shared with this wisdom's student so that, by the testimony of their conscience, the *name* of that wisdom's Initiator may remain preserved, thus fulfilling the saying, "Except the LORD

---

744   Hosea 1:10

of hosts had left unto us a very small remnant, we should have been as Sodom, and we should have been like unto Gomor'rah."[745] The continued existence and relevance of the living God's *name* depends upon that wisdom's offspring, for if they should fail to give what they have been given, and to explain what remains hidden from priests and ministers within the religious world, then conversations will suffer, spiritual negligence will advance as if sober understanding.

3. The entire point of the living God's confidence is to offer conversations an opportunity to possess a clean devotional mind to mindfully serve that philosophy's *name*, one's self, and other minds. This is why it says, "The end of the commandment is charity out of a pure heart, and of a good conscience, and of faith unfeigned."[746] Right charity is the aim of the Bible's faith, and because we cannot, without learning of and doing that commandment, "love one another, as he gave us commandment,"[747] we are counseled to prove the Bible's philosophy.[748]

4. True charity begins inwardly, with the person willing to not only acknowledge their devotional illness, but also to do something about it, saying, "Who shall deliver me from the body of this death?"[749] The "body" referenced is not the physical body, but is "the body of the sins of the flesh."[750] The "flesh" spoken of is the religious conversation, and the living God's intention is to regenerate and reform the conversation from "sin" against the *name* of the Bible's underlying confidence, and "sin" is presently identified as the religious law.[751] The "body of death" is a religious conversation bound to the religious law, but our faith is to be "written not with ink, but with the Spirit of the living God."[752]

5. This is why the doer of the Bible's confidence says, "The law of the Spirit of life in Christ Jesus hath made me free from the law of sin

---

745   Isaiah 1:9
746   1 Timothy 1:5
747   1 John 3:23
748   Romans 12:2
749   Romans 7:24
750   Colossians 2:11
751   1 Corinthians 15:56
752   2 Corinthians 3:3

and death."[753] The living God's righteousness is the living God's pleasure or fame. This fame is in resurrecting the conversation's conscience from "sin" against creation's present law to know harmony with that wisdom. The issue at hand is over the conversation's conscience and, "know ye not, brethren, (for I speak to them that know the law,) how that the law hath dominion over a man as long as he liveth?"[754]

6. The religious law halts right thinking and feeling by convincing its adherent to let "righteousness come by the law"[755] when, in reality, with the living God's chief apostle "having abolished in his flesh the enmity, even the law of commandments contained in ordinances,"[756] "the righteousness of God without the law is manifested."[757] With this man passed away on the tree, it is become a fact that his body represents what is accursed to the Bible's character, and since his conversation was "made under the law,"[758] his passing on the tree confirms that he "hath redeemed us from the curse of the law, being made a curse for us: for it is written, Cursed is every one that hangeth on a tree."[759]

7. With this man's body as a witness to the fact that "the strength of sin is the law,"[760] it is become evident that a resurrection in worship and service is preached. This is why he said, "Father, into thy hands I commend my spirit."[761] His dead body signifies the fact that the spirit of the mind is become the subject of creation, which is why he taught, "Be renewed in the spirit of your mind,"[762] and, "That which is born of the Spirit is spirit."[763] The religious conversation is to therefore find its heart and mind consecrated to this wisdom, for when numb to "sin" against the Bible's wisdom, wherein is there a mind to entertain religious error?

---

753 Romans 8:2
754 Romans 7:1
755 Galatians 2:21
756 Ephesians 2:15
757 Romans 3:21
758 Galatians 4:4
759 Galatians 3:13
760 1 Corinthians 15:56
761 Luke 23:46
762 Ephesians 4:23
763 John 3:6

8. "For in that he died, he died unto sin once: but in that he liveth, he liveth unto God";[764] it is our responsibility to "seek those things which are above, where Christ sitteth on the right hand of God."[765]

9. Seeing as how "God is a Spirit,"[766] and that "the Spirit of life"[767] is "the Word of life,"[768] to hear that this man lives unto *God* is to hear that this man possess a conversation wholly dedicated to salvation's science. And this fact the prophets repeatedly state, even as it is written, "He shall stand and feed in the strength of the LORD, in the majesty of the name of the LORD his God."[769] With this man's conversation passed away on the tree and then not only resurrected from the *death* of the tree, but found separated from the tree and brought into the living God's presence, what is preached to us is the counsel, "Put off concerning the former conversation the old man...and be renewed in the spirit of your mind."[770]

10. Herein is the charitable righteousness of the living God towards us, even the desire to "purge your conscience from dead works to serve the living God."[771] It is therefore fair to ask, "How is this purging to commence?" We receive our answer from how it says, "Who shall deliver me from the body of this death? I thank God through Jesus Christ our Lord."[772]

11. Because this baptism or sanctification is within the conscience, it is well to understand that Paul references no man or figure when saying, "Jesus Christ our Lord." In right context of language, "the Lord Jesus Christ our Saviour"[773] is "the commandment of God our Saviour,"[774] for by mentally and spiritually proving *salvation's* commandment, that natural "body" of "sin" is passed away, which is why Paul says, "With

---

764   Romans 6:10
765   Colossians 3:1
766   John 4:24
767   Revelation 11:11
768   1 John 1:1
769   Micah 5:4
770   Ephesians 4:22-24
771   Hebrews 9:14
772   Romans 7:24,25
773   Titus 1:4
774   Titus 1:3

the mind I myself serve the law of God,"[775] and, "I serve with my spirit in the gospel of his Son."[776]

12. Sanctification is "with the washing of water by the word,"[777] wherefore if failing to mentally and spiritually comprehend the Bible's present *voice*, the *body* of our faith will continue to adhere to "sin" as if it is not "sin," keeping our understanding "never able to come to the knowledge of the truth."[778] "Truth's" knowledge states, "The truth shall make you free,"[779] and if I, by this truth, should say, "The law of the Spirit of life in Christ Jesus hath made me free from the law of sin and death,"[780] it is evident that the living God's law and commandment is to reform my mind from what "sin" is, "and the strength of sin is the law."[781]

13. Again, the issue at hand is the government of the conversation and its conscience. If, by this slain man, the philosophy of the religious law is accursed and purged from the living God's character, and if the religious conversation is to be "perfect, as pertaining to the conscience,"[782] then subjection to the pen of theologians is not only a violation of the Bible's wisdom, but is also a violation of the conscience, making the person maintain a faith for the sake of doing so, and also for fear of punishment if not. This is a very inhumane way to devotionally function, which is why it says, "That through death he might... deliver them who through fear of death were all their lifetime subject to bondage."[783]

14. "The sting of death is sin; and the strength of sin is the law";[784] when hearing the phrase, "Fear of death," it is in reference to respect given to religious laws and doctrines of priests and elders. This reli-

---

775   Romans 7:25
776   Romans 1:9
777   Ephesians 5:26
778   2 Timothy 3:7
779   John 8:32
780   Romans 8:2
781   1 Corinthians 15:56
782   Hebrews 9:9
783   Hebrews 2:14,15
784   1 Corinthians 15:56

gious philosophy belongs to a contrary *wisdom*, wherefore the living God's minister, "having abolished in his flesh the enmity, even the law of commandments contained in ordinances,"[785] has for ever blotted out that contrary *philosophy* from the living God's *name*, deeming that contrary doctrine as "sin." To therefore hear a *Christ* preaching, "You are justified by the law,"[786] is to hear an imposter speaking against salvation's science, which science teaches, "By his knowledge shall my righteous servant justify many."[787]

15. The conversation's sanctification is the point of the Bible's will and wisdom, and sanctification, because "a spirit hath not flesh and bones,"[788] cannot commence in any place other than the spirit of the mind, which is why it says, "Worship God in the spirit,"[789] and, "That which is born of the Spirit is spirit."[790] As opposed to what "sanctifieth to the purifying of the flesh";[791] which is that routine nailed to the tree; the Bible's present commandment is ordained to "purge your conscience from dead works to serve the living God."[792] As the mind becomes acquainted with this intention, knowledge of "the law of truth"[793] will reveal to the heart the living God's intention, that we should be "full of goodness, filled with all knowledge, able also to admonish one another."[794]

16. As the mind, through *creation's* law, awakens from *death's* slumber take on a penitent character,[795] right love towards self will dawn upon the heart and the person, now discerning the Creator's benevolence, will begin to soberly care for self. This higher learning for our faith is so personal because the controversy is over self and self's government. The person must know that they are inwardly or

---

785   Ephesians 2:15
786   Galatians 5:4
787   Isaiah 53:11
788   Luke 24:39
789   Philippians 3:3
790   John 3:6
791   Hebrews 9:13
792   Hebrews 9:14
793   Malachi 2:6
794   Romans 15:14
795   Job 34:31,32

philosophically sick, and in a way to care for amendment, and the only way to do this is through inward discernment, which is why "we have received a commandment from the Father."[796]

17. Our mental, moral, spiritual, and physical health depends upon our compliance not only with justification's commandment, but also with that course of learning attached to it, which is why it says, "I wish above all things that thou mayest prosper and be in health, even as thy soul prospereth."[797] With the mind no longer relying on a confidence that is blotted out and abolished; "for whatsoever is not of faith is sin,"[798] "and the law is not of faith";[799] liberty of conscience may afford consciousness to the heart for realizing its worth, and for understanding the worth of every other heart.

18. By consenting to the Bible's present kindness, the person is taught where they fail to love themselves, and by applying to that wisdom to learn how to love self, knowledge of how to care for others will be given. With all of the skills and talents lent to that person by the Creator, they can then apply self in ways to celebrate the *name* that resurrected them, even as it is counseled, "Let every one of us please his neighbour for his good to edification."[800]

19. Because this manner of sanctification is through edification, when hearing the saying, "Love one another,"[801] it is that we are hearing, "Comfort yourselves together, and edify one another."[802] Whosoever is comforted by the living God's wisdom will comfort according to that wisdom's form of learning. This is why the course of the conversation's redemption is so inwardly taxing; the end of *creation's* law is a right mind executing right and sober charity.

20. Our Father has blessed this course of learning with a right manner of *love* for us to benevolently care for one another. This kindness is not the service of the religious world, but is actually a living

---

796   2 John 1:4
797   3 John 1:2
798   Romans 14:23
799   Galatians 3:12
800   Romans 15:2
801   1 Thessalonians 4:9
802   1 Thessalonians 5:11

remedy that must be given through exactly what is observed. Any mishandling of this wisdom will only inflame our natural devotional sickness, which is why, to best advise against this sickness, and to best help treat it, a commandment for our conversation's course of learning has been given.

21. This sanctification is the key to our ministry. If not sanctified by the knowledge of the living God's chief apostle, do we not but preach "philosophy and vain deceit, after the tradition of men, after the rudiments of the world"?[803] What separates the *son* of the Bible's wisdom from the disciple of the religious world is the aim and will of their service. While the *earth* preaches the imprisonment of the mind through "Jewish fables, and commandments of men, that turn from the truth,"[804] the Bible counsels, "Live according to God in the spirit."[805]

22. Care for the human and the devotional condition, along with their experience, is at the heart of the Bible's philosophy, wherefore the amendment of the conversation's mind is the key to the person properly demonstrating charity. This discipline, for the perpetual remembrance of the living God's *name*, and for the wellbeing of other conversations, is for us to help others less fortunate in mind and in confidence, and to encourage others already engaged in *creation's* law. Every conversation resurrected by the Bible's wisdom ought to then never forget that we all do look for edification to live by.

---

803 Colossians 2:8
804 Titus 1:14
805 1 Peter 4:6

26

Compassion's Task

1. For every mind trained in creation's science, it is our responsibility to properly care for those minds without knowledge of "the kindness and love of God our Saviour toward man."[806] Knowledge of this wisdom means nothing if it is not used to properly bless the inwards of another conversation, to the end that conversation may not only regain strength, but also do for another what has been done for it. We learn this benevolence from how one once said, "If thou canst do any thing, have compassion on us, and help us."[807] What was the response? It says, "He rebuked the foul spirit."[808]

2. To the Bible's mind, "compassion" is an act of comforting the spirit of the mind. "Comfort" is learning; it says, "All may learn, and all

---

806 Titus 3:4
807 Mark 9:22
808 Mark 9:25

may be comforted."[809] If we "are taught of God to love one another,"[810] then it is that we honor the counsel, "Comfort yourselves together, and edify one another, even as also ye do."[811] "Compassion," "comfort," and "learning," these all are, to the Bible's mind, the definition of "love," which "love" is mental and spiritual edification. This is why it says, "Let every one of us please his neighbour for his good to edification."[812]

3. "God" is to be acknowledged as the Bible's *Word* or *Wisdom*, seeing as how "in the beginning...the Word was God."[813] If it is that our faith's mind is taught by the *Word*, it is that, by that course of learning, the character of this wisdom's heart will find itself engraved upon our thoughts and feelings, moving our person to care for edifying according to the same manner and impression given by that same *Word*. This wisdom's will is the revival and reformation of the personal devotional conversation, and to execute this redemption, regeneration must commence within the conversation's conscience.[814] This is why "we have received a commandment from the Father."[815]

4. Because our conversation is "to be strengthened with might by his Spirit in the inner man,"[816] since "wisdom strengtheneth,"[817] it is that the Bible's present commandment is to be our faith's educator and comforter, which is why it says, "The Comforter, which is the Holy Ghost...he shall teach you all things."[818] The living God's manner of "love" is through educating the inwards of the conversation, and we fall in to that love by examining and doing that commandment for mental and spiritual newness, which is why it says, "Be renewed in the spirit of your mind."[819]

---

809   1 Corinthians 14:31
810   1 Thessalonians 4:9
811   1 Thessalonians 5:11
812   Romans 15:2
813   John 1:1
814   Hebrews 9:14
815   2 John 1:4
816   Ephesians 3:16
817   Ecclesiastes 7:19
818   John 14:26
819   Ephesians 4:23

5. Herein is heaven-appointed "compassion," and if taught and comforted by the Bible's mind, it is our responsibility to encourage the renewing of other minds. The living God's chief apostle demonstrated compassion by no carnal or sensual means, but by alleviating the character of an individual's spirit. "Spirit"; as is evident from Paul's language, which says, "The spirit of your mind";[820] is mind. An unclean spirit, in right context, is a mind disturbed by a specific religious understanding or doctrine, which perplexity can cast the conversation's heart, if not properly guarded, "into the fire, and into the waters, to destroy."[821]

6. This "fire" is no literal fire, but is according to the saying, "Whose fire is in Zion, and his furnace in Jerusalem."[822] This "fire" is to be thought of as a "furnace," and this "furnace," if in "Zion," is according to the saying, "The law shall go forth of Zion, and the word of the LORD from Jerusalem."[823]

7. To be cast in to the "fire" is to be cast in to the furnace of a specific word or doctrine, which furnace is that of *Egypt's* religious understanding, as it says, "I brought them forth out of the land of Egypt, from the iron furnace."[824] The "waters" to find self cast in to are also no literal destination; "the waters...are peoples, and multitudes, and nations, and tongues."[825] These "waters" of religious denominations are the "sea"; "the gathering together of the waters called he Seas";[826] and the doctrine of the religious world is a contrary religious philosophy, as it says, "The dragon that is in the sea."[827]

8. That furnace for the unclean spirit, being the religious persuasion of *Egypt*, also possesses the *dragon's* superstition, for it says of Egypt's spiritual leader, "Pharaoh king of Egypt, the great dragon."[828] Thus, an

---

820   Ephesians 4:23
821   Mark 9:22
822   Isaiah 31:9
823   Micah 4:2
824   Jeremiah 11:4
825   Revelation 17:15
826   Genesis 1:10
827   Isaiah 27:1
828   Ezekiel 29:3

unclean spirit is recognized by its desire to turn to that "God" of the "furnace" of "waters" for explanations, which only further inflames the disease within the mind, for the *dragon* has no right answer or record of the living God's wisdom.

9. Concerning this *dragon*, "he was cast out into the earth,"[829] and concerning the location of his *faith*, he says, "From going to and fro in the earth."[830] It is then no wonder why the mind remains unclean and unclear when turned to the spirit of the religious world, for if it says, "For ever, O LORD, thy word is settled in heaven,"[831] if, instead of extending our mind heavenward we plunge in to the *earth's* core, must we not expect devotional anxiety? The unclean mind remains unclean because of its spiritual diet, and the more our conversation's conscience remains without *heaven's* fresh air, the more perverse the Bible's *voice* and impression will become, until fulfilling the saying, "God shall send them strong delusion...that they all might be damned who believed not the truth, but had pleasure in unrighteousness."[832]

10. Because the *dragon's* contrary wisdom rules the *air* or the atmosphere of the religious world, it is that its philosophy is against *heaven's* fresh *air*, even striving to blot out the sight of *heaven* and to pollute its air by the smoke released from its furnace. This contrary creed is in all "unrighteousness," and "all unrighteousness is sin,"[833] "and the strength of sin is the law."[834] The dragon's religion is based upon that philosophy and ideology nailed to the tree, and with the living God's man "having abolished in his flesh the enmity, even the law of commandments contained in ordinances,"[835] it is become a fact that "the strength of sin is the law."[836]

---

829 Revelation 12:9
830 Job 1:7
831 Psalm 119:89
832 2 Thessalonians 2:11,12
833 1 John 5:17
834 1 Corinthians 15:56
835 Ephesians 2:15
836 1 Corinthians 15:56

11. To be "damned" is to be "accursed" or "condemned," and if it says, "He that is hanged is accursed of God,"[837] then what is accursed belongs to what the body of the living God's minister represents, which is a conversation strengthened by the religious law. This priest, figuratively "blotting out the handwriting of ordinances"[838] through his passing on the tree, has condemned the religious law as "sin." The conversation therefore accursed of the *Word* and bearing an unclean spirit is in that condition because the *eyes* of their understanding are not fixed on "those things which are above, where Christ sitteth on the right hand of God."[839]

12. With the condemnation of that religious body, the tree stands as a perpetual sign of alienation from the living God's *throne* and its philosophy, but with the conversation of this man separated from the tree and found as "a great high priest, that is passed into the heavens,"[840] what is preached is the regeneration of the conversation's conscience from the *wisdom* of the *dragon* to the living God's wisdom. This is why it says, "To open their eyes, and to turn them from darkness to light, and from the power of Satan unto God."[841] Herein is witnessed "the kindness and love of God our Saviour toward man,"[842] even the healing of our faith's heart and mind to know the intended resurrection.[843]

13. Redemption is for the conversation. This redemption occurs only as the mind is edified by the Bible's present *voice*, which is why it is counseled, "Be ye transformed by the renewing of your mind, that ye may prove what is that good, and acceptable, and perfect, will of God."[844] For this cause, every spirit blessed to enter into faith's higher learning, and while learning of and experiencing this benevolence, will be encouraged and pleased to care for others after the manner of this rehabilitation.

---

837   Deuteronomy 21:23
838   Colossians 2:14
839   Colossians 3:1
840   Hebrews 4:14
841   Acts 26:18
842   Titus 3:4
843   Philippians 3:10
844   Romans 12:2

14. Because our conversation is naturally born from a religious world sinning against the living God's *name*, it is well for the one mentally escaped in to the heavenly Sanctuary, and through the knowledge of the living God's chief minister, to return to them that are "in bondage under the elements of the world,"[845] to aid their conversation's ascension into the *Building* of higher learning. The unclean spirit is easily recognized by their *water* and *fire* marks, and to such as wrestle against the Bible's influence, it is that we who are members of that Building ought to do what we can to restore their conversation.[846]

15. This father approaching the living God's minister was concerned for his son in the faith. His son was having great difficulty comprehending just what the scriptures taught. It was because of his poor *diet* that his mind was "tossed to and fro, and carried about with every wind of doctrine, by the sleight of men, and cunning craftiness, whereby they lie in wait to deceive."[847]

16. A grand chasm, established "through philosophy and vain deceit, after the tradition of men,"[848] had formed to separate his mind from the living God's influence, but when hearing this minister soberly pronounce what his heart desired, his faith came together, but not after criticizing his thoughts.[849] Herein is pronounced to us the height of compassion, even the vocation of alleviating another's conversation to initiate a personal philosophical revival. This compassion is to lead to one arising from the *death* of religious error to receive new breath within the spirit of their mind, which is why it says, "That which is born of the Spirit is spirit."[850]

17. It is therefore our responsibility, as student-patients of the living God's higher education, to become an educational servant to whoever is troubled and sincerely cares for understanding how to heal self. This man's mind was not easy to edify, but the living God's chief apostle

---

845   Galatians 4:3
846   Galatians 6:1
847   Ephesians 4:14
848   Colossians 2:8
849   Mark 9:26,27
850   John 3:6

did not leave him, and when he was at his lowest, he was there to assist and serve his regeneration. The living God's man, to better this man's condition, did not do any *thing* but speak the Bible's saying to him. The troubled minister experienced liberty by taking knowledge of what was spoken, and by exercising faith on that saying, and on the virtue of the *voice* pronouncing that saying.

18. We do not help any one by being their ears, or their hands, or their eyes, or their mouth, or their mind, or their *body*. Is the Bible's wisdom become our body, our ears, or our mind? Isn't it written, "Of his own will begat he us with the word of truth"?[851] The Bible's manner of edifying is mental and inward discernment, allowing the person to add consciousness to their faith's mind, mouth, body, and organs, after personally handling its words.

19. This consciousness is the means whereby our faith blesses both the mental and physical government of our person, keeping us in fit shape to soberly bless that resurrecting wisdom, our self, and other minds. The living God's utterance must be given in a way for the mind of the person to think on it for learning how to bless their own perception, which is why his man only spoke the revelation, and at the time appointed, assisted the person, for he would not always be around, just as we are not always around the ones we *comfort*.

20. The student of the Bible is born and trained to encourage and heal conversations; if we cannot be patient with our self when passing through this course of learning, must we think to be patient with another? Isn't it written, "The servant of the Lord must not strive; but be gentle unto all men, apt to teach, patient, in meekness instructing those that oppose themselves"?[852]

21. If our conversation, which naturally opposes the Bible's devotional character, is not educated by its science against opposition, and do hope to shed right *light* on conversation's contrary to that mind and science, should we not lead them further in to opposition if we are not disciplined? Our counsel will lay on that person in a very sore way,

---

851   James 1:18
852   2 Timothy 2:24-26

moving them to know the *fire* of certain *waters* for destroying the very *life* they have. But if we are patient with self to learn *creation's voice*, we open up our heart to perceive its confidence, increasing our faith to not only remain inwardly quiet, but to also become teachable.

22. Every heart prays, "That which I see not teach thou me,"[853] therefore it is well to cultivate a temperate and patient spirit through learning of and doing *creation's* present will. Our conversation should turn away no hopeful mind, but should accept every conversation willing to learn and do. Being first trained by the Bible, our conversation must comfort and edify as it has been comforted and edified.

---

853   Job 34:32

27

Edification's Private Learning

1. There is a point to faith's higher education. The conversation faithful to the Bible's present course of learning will receive employment specifically tailored to their person, which vocation revolves around the saying, "My lips shall utter praise, when thou hast taught me thy statutes."[854] Only when our person is taught by the living God's *name* can our lips utter beneficial praise. This is why it says, "The end of the commandment is charity out of a pure heart, and of a good conscience, and of faith unfeigned."[855]

2. It is written, "In the lips of him that hath understanding wisdom is found."[856] It says this because faith's classroom will train the conversation on right wisdom, to live by it, that it may soberly give the

854   Psalm 119:171
855   1 Timothy 1:5
856   Proverbs 10:13

revelation of that wisdom to minds that should know it. The Bible's course of learning is for cultivating a ministry according to the specific gifts and talents we are born with, but in order to be a blessing, it is that those gifts and talents, along with our conversation's character, must experience its science. It is only after our conversation is brought up in Bible wisdom that we may claim our ministry. Our training has taught us how to connect to the mediation of the Bible's confidence, and by possessing self through that will, our faith's *mouth* will utter the wisdom of its intercession.

3. The ministry of *creation's* steward is devoted to the will of the living God's "Word" or "Wisdom"; "My meat is to do the will of him that sent me, and to finish his work,"[857] they say. Isn't it that this same man says, "As my Father hath sent me, even so send I you"?[858] Like as "the Son of man came not to be ministered unto, but to minister, and to give his life a ransom for many,"[859] so too the Bible's steward has the assignment of strengthening their conversation to share it with many, and "wisdom strengtheneth."[860]

4. The confidence of the living God's chief apostle was not found within the religious world, which is why it says, "He that is spiritual judgeth all things, yet he himself is judged of no man."[861] To be "judged" of *men* is to have the conversation ruled by the pen of priests and elders, but this man possessed a mind saying, "Why is my liberty judged of another man's conscience?"[862] Greater than "the handwriting of ordinances"[863] is inward and philosophical sobriety, which is why he said, "I know him, and keep his saying."[864] "That which is born of the Spirit is spirit,"[865] and if "of his own will begat he us with the word of

---

857 John 4:34
858 John 20:21
859 Mark 10:45
860 Ecclesiastes 7:19
861 1 Corinthians 2:15
862 1 Corinthians 10:29
863 Colossians 2:14
864 John 8:55
865 John 3:6

truth,"[866] then this man, seeing as how we are "to be strengthened with might by his Spirit in the inner man,"[867] was *born* through the spirit of his mind.

5. The living God's chief minister kept and experienced the saying of the wisdom within the scriptures, and by bringing that knowledge hidden within the scriptures into his mind, daily proving that understanding, the living God's will and doctrine became so pronounced to his heart that he confessed, "Princes also did sit and speak against me: but thy servant did meditate in thy statutes,"[868] and, "Princes have persecuted me without a cause: but my heart standeth in awe of thy word."[869]

6. This man's conversation wasn't born for institutionalized instruction; "The Son of man came not to be ministered unto,"[870] it says. By keeping and dressing his conversation with the Bible's wisdom, the wisdom he obtained blessed whosoever came in to contact with it, and this discipline is not held only to him, which is why he says, "Hereafter ye shall see heaven open, and the angels of God ascending and descending upon the Son of man."[871]

7. He was educated from out of *heaven*. Concerning "heaven," how it is defined, it says, "He hath looked down from the height of his sanctuary; from heaven did the LORD behold the earth."[872]

8. To hear, "I came down from heaven,"[873] is not to hear of any literal dissent from any celestial location, but to hear one confessing that, after their education within the *heavenly Sanctuary*, or after being trained by the wisdom within the scriptures, they obtained blessing to execute a ministry within the religious world. What went up and came down from "heaven" was a mind, which is why "that which is born of

---

866   James 1:18
867   Ephesians 3:16
868   Psalm 119:23
869   Psalm 119:161
870   Mark 10:45
871   John 1:51
872   Psalm 102:19
873   John 6:42

the Spirit is spirit,"[874] and why John reports that he saw "the Spirit descending, and remaining on him."[875]

9. What exists within the *heavenly Sanctuary* is the living God's *Word* or *Wisdom*, which is why it says, "For ever, O LORD, thy word is settled in heaven."[876] Seeing as how words are not firstly physical, and that "a spirit hath not flesh and bones,"[877] it is that a specific "body" is ordained to commune with the *temple* above, and "God giveth it a body as it hath pleased him."[878] Thus, since "that which is born of the Spirit is spirit,"[879] it says, "Be renewed in the spirit of your mind,"[880] which is advice to "worship God in the spirit."[881] Herein the living God's minister establishes an example for our faith's learning, whose conversation has ascended and is become our faith's instructor.

10. If it is that the living God's man says, "As my Father hath sent me, even so send I you,"[882] it is a fact that both the mission and education of his conversation is become our own. With his man "blotting out the handwriting of ordinances,"[883] it is that knowledge of his *name*, without the inspiration of the pen of theologians, remains for our handling, moving us to say, "With me it is a very small thing that I should be judged of you, or of man's judgment: yea, I judge not mine own self."[884] Knowledge of the Bible's confidence, and a sober comprehension of it is, by the act of this man on the tree, all that should matter to our personal devotional conversation. "Having abolished in his flesh the enmity, even the law of commandments contained in ordinances,"[885]

---

874   John 3:6
875   John 1:33
876   Psalm 119:89
877   Luke 24:39
878   1 Corinthians 15:38
879   John 3:6
880   Ephesians 4:23
881   Philippians 3:3
882   John 20:21
883   Colossians 2:14
884   1 Corinthians 4:13
885   Ephesians 2:15

he has openly defined "sin" against *heaven's* new covenant course of learning, "and the strength of sin is the law."[886]

11. The "judgment" or pen of priests and ministers is "sin" to the cause of the Bible's will and wisdom, and the living God's chief minister preached this fact by how he carried his conversation. His ministry is born "to redeem them that were under the law"[887] for the regeneration of their conversation's conscience. If the mind must examine and prove the Bible's science, no platform of learning must exist to that mind other than that platform found above the *earth*. With the mind willingly separated from the wisdom of the religious world, the conversation has the opportunity to receive consciousness by the consciousness blessed to its conscience: this is "the kindness and love of God our Saviour toward man."[888]

12. The living God's will for the conversation to benevolently possess self for *creation's* philosophy, self, and for the good of other minds is for the doer of the Bible's present *name*. That "good" for both self and others is that "love" of the living Creator. If our conversation is "taught of God to love one another,"[889] it is that we know how it says, "Comfort yourselves together, and edify one another."[890]

13. "Love," to the Bible, is mental and spiritual edification, which is why the conversation descending from *heaven* is counseled, "Seek that ye may excel to the edifying of the church,"[891] and, "Let every one of us please his neighbour for his good to edification."[892] *Heaven's* steward is trained to edify and to educate according to *heaven's* manner of comfort, even as it says, "Love one another, as he gave us commandment."[893]

---

886   1 Corinthians 15:56
887   Galatians 4:5
888   Titus 3:4
889   1 Thessalonians 4:9
890   1 Thessalonians 5:11
891   1 Corinthians 14:12
892   Romans 15:2
893   1 John 3:23

14. The Bible's form of love is a will that our inwards "be filled with the knowledge of his will in all wisdom and spiritual understanding."[894] In order to obtain knowledge on the Bible's mind, it is that the devotional conscience must patiently and temperately review its words, which is why it says, "In his law doth he meditate day and night."[895]

15. By learning of doing the living God's *voice*, knowledge of its intention informs the heart of its character, enlightening the perception it has of its person. This "spirit of wisdom and revelation in the knowledge of him"[896] is the key to our becoming familiar with the new covenant's intention. There is a goal to such a strict educational learning, and it is to fulfill the saying, "I will give them one heart, and one way, that they may fear me for ever."[897]

16. It is crucial that our faith's will is synonymous with *heaven's* will because the ministry we uphold is to be in devotion to *heaven's* philosophy, as it says, "Every tongue should confess that Jesus Christ is Lord, to the glory of God the Father,"[898] and, "Unto him be glory in the church by Christ Jesus throughout all ages."[899] If it is that our speech should reference this wisdom, it is that our conversation must become creations of this wisdom. Creation is *heaven's* intention, and creation through a specific course of learning for a peculiar vocation. *Heaven's* steward is to knowledgeably give *creation's* science, and if not a partaker of that benevolence, must we think to edify according to its commandment?

17. "We have received a commandment from the Father"[900] to learn how to possess self for soberly caring for that commandment's *name*, for correctly caring for the conversation, and for justly caring for other minds. Right charity does not begin with an outward act, but with self patiently and temperately comforting its thoughts and feelings. The Bible's wisdom is ordained to impute consciousness to the mind for

---

894 Colossians 1:9
895 Psalm 1:2
896 Ephesians 1:17
897 Jeremiah 32:39
898 Philippians 2:11
899 Ephesians 3:21
900 2 John 1:4

experiencing the righteousness, or the rightness, of that wisdom, which righteousness states: "Like as Christ was raised up from the dead by the glory of the Father, even so we also should walk in newness of life."[901]

18. The "life" is the personal religious conversation. Newness of mind is preached through *heaven's* new covenant will for a perfect conversation, and "perfect, as pertaining to the conscience."[902] The mind is to receive a faith to live by, and this reception is by mentally and spiritually consuming the Bible's current *saying*. This newly developing faith is to replace our old or former confidence, crucifying it, to the end we may boldly say, "Father, into thy hands I commend my spirit."[903] Hereafter our former devotional mind is put away so that our conversation can obtain a right experience. [904] Again, "the strength of sin is the law,"[905] and with the mind refraining from the pen of theologians to know and keep "the law of the Spirit of life,"[906] our *body* of faith has the chance to shed the skin of its natural understanding for dawning a sanctified *form*.

19. The intention is to learn of the Bible's will without the support and stimulus of a flesh-based practice, and to know that our faith advances not through the handwritten religious law, but through exercising confidence on the living God's wisdom.[907] A complete reform in personal devotional thought and feeling is then necessary in order to experience the Bible's benevolence; the mind must be free from "bondage under the elements of the world."[908]

20. What binds the conversation's heart will stop the person from exercising faith for understanding, "for whatsoever is not of faith is sin,"[909] "and the law is not of faith."[910] Understanding that the religious

---

901   Romans 6:4
902   Hebrews 9:9
903   Luke 23:46
904   Romans 6:6
905   1 Corinthians 15:56
906   Romans 8:2
907   2 Corinthians 3:5,6
908   Galatians 4:3
909   Romans 14:23
910   Galatians 3:12

law is "sin" against the Bible's discipline, it will be put away for a better rule of government, which rule forwards the confession, "The law of the Spirit of life in Christ Jesus hath made me free from the law of sin and death."[911] This liberty of conscience opens up the mind to learn in new ways, impressing upon the heart a desire to care for self after observing how the living Father cares for them.

21. Love attracts love, and as the inwards of our conversation are edified by the Bible's wisdom and character, it will be that we will care to rightly learn how to care for our own self, and how to also properly edify another. There is no thing more valuable than mentally perceiving injury and that injury's consolation. Right benevolent affection for another is born when the mind clearly discerns its damaging error, for then the aim of betterment is not vain, being similar to "them which glory in appearance, and not in heart."[912]

22. Mental activity is the prerequisite to the Bible's appointed intention because the mind must be convinced not only of wrong or right, but of its responsibility to consistently revive and reform from wrong to right, even as it says, "Lest they see with their eyes, and hear with their ears, and understand with their heart, and convert, and be healed."[913] True conversion begins within the heart, and that beginning is forwarded by what the ears *hear*.

23. What is heard is blessed by what the eyes discern. This is in no way a reference to your literal eyes, but rather to "the eyes of your understanding."[914] Charity begins when once the *eyes* of our faith's confidence are edified by the wisdom of the living God's will, which is why his chief minister says, "I know him, and keep his saying."[915] This saying prepared him for a public ministry by blessing the private ministry he devoted to his character's inward conversation, which is why it says of him, "This is my beloved Son: hear him."[916]

---

911   Romans 8:2
912   2 Corinthians 5:12
913   Isaiah 6:10
914   Ephesians 1:18
915   John 8:55
916   Mark 9:7

24. Our journey begins within the *heavenly Sanctuary*, and then if we are faithful to that experience, we will receive the privilege of joining *heaven's priesthood* for turning *eyes* heavenward. The conversation blessed to give their *life* for the edifying of minds is in that office for the hardship they've internally faced, and do still face, but privately.

25. When alone, we only have our mind to counsel, but outside of our mind are minds plagued by all sorts of *sores* and *diseases*, and who may not care to know the state of their faith's existence, or lack thereof. The Bible's ministry is very specific to the human condition; it resurrects what is "contrary to nature into a good olive tree."[917] If our conversation has not experienced this resurrection, the knowledge of this redemption will not proceed from our lips, but rather a self-concocted delusion "to make the Gentiles obedient, by word and deed."[918]

26. To be rightly charitable, it is that our conversation must know the Bible's manner of charity. Salvation's student must, by the testimony of this benevolence engraved upon their conscience, utter the praise of this philosophy's wisdom. When once we are, through "rightly dividing the word of truth,"[919] taught of *heaven's* wisdom by *heaven's* mind, our praise will, seeing as how our *voice* has endured the living God's furnace to become a perfect illustration of that wisdom within *heaven's* Building, be ready for the public.

---

917   Romans 11:24
918   Romans 15:18
919   2 Timothy 2:15

28

Resurrection's Intention

1. When thinking on just what the "resurrection from the dead" should mean, and on how to define the "dead," it is well to hear how it says, "The first begotten of the dead, and the prince of the kings of the earth,"[920] and, "It stirreth up the dead for thee, even all the chief ones of the earth."[921] The "dead" are the "kings of the earth," and a "king," in context, is a term denoting a "priest," even as it says, "And hath made us kings and priests unto God and his Father."[922]

2. These "kings" and "chief ones" are chief priests and ministers of denominations; we learn this from how it says, "They shall lay their hands on you, and persecute you, delivering you up to the synagogues, and into prisons, being brought before kings and rulers for my name's

---

920   Revelation 1:5
921   Isaiah 14:9
922   Revelation 1:6

171

sake."[923] The "resurrection from the dead" is then a purging of the conversation from the pen and spirit of priests and elders, and this is what is referenced through the living God's chief apostle, in that it says, "Like as Christ was raised up from the dead by the glory of the Father, even so we also should walk in newness of life."[924]

3. When speaking on that "body" to suffer destruction and regeneration, "he spake of the temple of his body."[925] This means that the "glory" raising up this man was "the Spirit of him that raised up Jesus from the dead,"[926] and seeing as how "a spirit hath not flesh and bones,"[927] we cannot think that this *Spirit* should raise up flesh, especially since "that which is born of the Spirit is spirit."[928] It is the temple of this man's conversation that was destroyed and rebuilt, and if rebuilt of the *Spirit*, it is that the spirit of his mind became separated from the mind of *men*.

4. This minister was naturally "made under the law,"[929] but then "was made a quickening spirit,"[930] "being put to death in the flesh, but quickened by the Spirit."[931] This slain temple and body is no literal or physical *thing*, but is the flesh or body of his faith's confidence. What makes this *temple's* destruction so significant is that while the fashion of *men* upheld this *body*, "the Word was made flesh";[932] herein two minds dwelt within one conversation. Thus, "having abolished in his flesh the enmity, even the law of commandments contained in ordinances,"[933] the illustration of this man's crucifixion for ever pronounces the fact that "the sting of death is sin; and the strength of sin is the law."[934]

---

923   Luke 21:12
924   Romans 6:4
925   John 2:21
926   Romans 8:11
927   Luke 24:39
928   John 3:6
929   Galatians 4:4
930   1 Corinthians 15:45
931   1 Peter 3:18
932   John 1:14
933   Ephesians 2:15
934   1 Corinthians 15:56

5. "Death's" course is today understood as a conversation fastened and forwarded by "the law of commandments contained in ordinances,"[935] making that conversation, by this man's crucified body, "sinful." What was slain on the tree was the religious fashion of priests and elders, which fashion states, "Their fear toward me is taught by the precept of men,"[936] and, "Full well ye reject the commandment of God, that ye may keep your own tradition."[937] "Philosophy and vain deceit, after the tradition of men, after the rudiments of the world,"[938] is the confidence of priests and ministers, but with this minister "blotting out the handwriting of ordinances,"[939] that persuasion by the pen of theologians is made to give up the *ghost* while the fact of the wisdom within the scriptures fills up our faith's *body*.

6. This explains what that "resurrection" from the "dead" is. If the "dead" are the chief *men*, and if these chief ministers are "dead" for their subscription to that abolished form of devotion, then the "resurrection" from the "dead" is mental and spiritual redemption from the manners of priests and elders, from the philosophy of the religious world. And isn't this what is written? Doesn't it say, "Be dead with Christ from the rudiments of the world"?[940] Isn't it written of the "dead," "They are the enemies of the cross of Christ...who mind earthly things"?[941]

7. What does it mean to be an enemy of the cross but to transgress the definition behind the illustration of the crucifixion? The illustration is plain, for it says, "Having abolished in his flesh the enmity, even the law of commandments contained in ordinances."[942] The "flesh" of the man represents what "sin" is, and "the sting of death is sin; and the strength of sin is the law";[943] the one honoring this illustration's defini-

---

935   Ephesians 1:15
936   Isaiah 29:13
937   Mark 7:9
938   Colossians 2:8
939   Colossians 2:14
940   Colossians 2:20
941   Philippians 3:18,19
942   Ephesians 2:15
943   1 Corinthians 15:56

tion will say, "The law of the Spirit of life in Christ Jesus hath made me free from the law of sin and death."[944] Such a statement witnesses to the point of the illustration, that "he that is hanged is accursed of God."[945]

8. With the flesh of this man representing the philosophy of the religious law, what is become cursed and condemned is the pen of priests and elders; "Christ hath redeemed us from the curse of the law, being made a curse for us: for it is written, Cursed is every one that hangeth on a tree."[946] Thus, by this man, "death's" religion is become known by its use of "the law of commandments contained in ordinances,"[947] and because the only ones favoring this religious philosophy are the priests and preachers within the religious world, it is that the "resurrection from the dead" is a separation of devotional thought and feeling from them that "profess that they know God; but in works they deny him."[948]

9. By not only adhering to "the handwriting of ordinances,"[949] but also inventing and forwarding "the law of commandments contained in ordinances,"[950] blatant transgression against the living God's present dispensation is committed. If that dispensation's ministry is blessed "to redeem them that were under the law,"[951] yet all say that "you are justified by the law,"[952] "if righteousness come by the law, then Christ is dead in vain."[953] And not only is this man's death in vain, but such religious error is against the illustration of his own offering, making *him* an advocate for what is abolished, fulfilling the saying, "They crucify to themselves the Son of God afresh, and put him to an open shame."[954]

10. The living God's man on the tree is a witness to the presently irrelevant nature of the tree, for the tree and the philosophy nailed to it

---

944   Romans 8:2
945   Deuteronomy 21:23
946   Galatians 3:13
947   Ephesians 2:15
948   Titus 1:16
949   Colossians 2:14
950   Ephesians 2:15
951   Galatians 4:5
952   Galatians 5:4
953   Galatians 2:21
954   Hebrews 6:6

is, to the Bible's mind, because the crucified is accursed,[955] without any living force. In order to find *blessing* by the tree, a forced interpretation of the scriptures must be applied. What is preached through this man on the tree is a crucifixion of one mind of devotion for the regeneration of a new mind of devotion. This is why, although that *ghost* of religious error is condemned, he prayed, before passing, "Father, into thy hands I commend my spirit."[956]

11. What is observed through the illustration of the crucifixion is a complete passing away from *death's* persuasion to draw nearer to the living God's mind of devotion. The "resurrection from the dead" is a spiritual recovery "from your vain conversation received by tradition,"[957] to the end the conversation may know the certainty of every word within the Bible. And we understand that we honor this risen confidence because it says, "He was known of them in breaking of bread."[958]

12. "Bread" is another term for "doctrine," as it says, "He bade them not beware of the leaven of bread, but of the doctrine of the Pharisees and of the Sadducees."[959] To break bread is to break or to examine doctrine. If this man's *name* were not separated from the spirit of his conversation, there would be no advancing knowledge on his *name's* wisdom. It therefore became clear to the first apostles that this confidence is that wisdom because, although condemned to physical death, this wisdom existed without or beyond the man's death, and for "knowledge of his will in all wisdom and spiritual understanding."[960]

13. If his conversation's character did not further pronounce its doctrine to the initial apostles, their weeping would have continued, but when this wisdom manifested to their conscience, it "upbraided them with their unbelief and hardness of heart, because they believed not them which had seen him after he was risen."[961] "Then opened he

---

955   Deuteronomy 21:23
956   Luke 23:46
957   1 Peter 1:18
958   Luke 24:35
959   Matthew 16:12
960   Colossians 1:9
961   Mark 16:14

their understanding, that they might understand the scriptures,"[962] and "breathed on them, and saith unto them, Receive ye the Holy Ghost."[963]

14. Remember how it says, "That which is born of the Spirit is spirit"?[964] The reception of the *Spirit* is the same as opening up the understanding to comprehending the scriptures; this is why our conversation is "to be strengthened with might by his Spirit in the inner man."[965] The living God's *Spirit* is received within the inwards of the conversation, and that reception, as explained by Luke, is through mentally reviewing words, which is why it says, "I will pour out my spirit unto you, I will make known my words unto you."[966] Herein we may understand that, after the man died, the "appearing" witnessed by the first apostles was no literal or physical appearing, but was a revelation by the spirit of their mind from "rightly dividing the word of truth,"[967] even as it says, "Gird up the loins of your mind, be sober, and hope to the end for the grace that is to be brought unto you at the revelation of Jesus Christ."[968]

15. Again, Peter explains to us that this revelation is mental, allowing us to know that "Jesus Christ" is no reference to any physical *thing*. "The Lord Jesus Christ our Saviour"[969] is, in all actuality, and according to the context and the placement of the words within this phrase, "the commandment of God our Saviour."[970] Thus, the revelation of "Jesus Christ" is, in reality, the revelation of the living God's present commandment, which is why it is important to hear that, when perceiving this commandment, the first apostles received the *Spirit* because "that which is born of the Spirit is spirit."[971]

16. This reception is to the spirit of the conversation's mind, for by examining the Bible's words, knowledge of the fact that this wisdom

---

962   Luke 24:45
963   John 20:22
964   John 3:6
965   Ephesians 3:16
966   Proverbs 1:23
967   2 Timothy 2:15
968   1 Peter 1:13
969   Titus 1:4
970   Titus 1:3
971   John 3:6

transcends the religious world dawned upon them. This man then became "risen" in the same sense that John was risen from the dead, for it was not that the human being was among them, but rather that the wisdom of that doctrine and commandment preached by the man overshadowed their heart.

17. With knowledge of this man's *name* continuing to feed their spiritual understanding, it was known and understood that this is that risen charge of the living God, and that it had "spoiled principalities and powers"[972] that forwarded "the perfect manner of the law of the fathers."[973] Hereafter every sincere conversation learning of and doing this commandment would hear, "Put off concerning the former conversation the old man...and be renewed in the spirit of your mind."[974] An evident reform in manners of worship and service then became known to the first apostles, for they could not receive *heaven's* new covenant intention while remaining faithful to "the tradition of the elders,"[975] which is why it says, "We who are Jews by nature...even we have believed in Jesus Christ, that we might be justified by the faith of Christ, and not by the works of the law."[976]

18. What convinced the apostles of this man's risen state was the fact that his doctrine condemned the use of the religious law but advocated creation by faith on his conversation's *voice*. This man's doctrine is the living God's will and benevolence, and what halts its kind benefit is a practice refusing to learn how to exercise faith for knowledge, teaching us that "whatsoever is not of faith is sin,"[977] and that "the law is not of faith."[978]

19. Because the religious law is without faith's higher learning, it must be taken out of the living God's course of learning and removed from the personal conversation, for it is written, "By his knowledge

---

972   Colossians 2:15
973   Acts 22:3
974   Ephesians 4:22,23
975   Matthew 15:2
976   Galatians 2:15,16
977   Romans 14:23
978   Galatians 3:12

shall my righteous servant justify many."[979] While the "dead" preach, "You are justified by the law,"[980] such speech is witnessed to be injurious according to the fact that justification; which is sanctification; is by no handwritten religious law, but is by an experimental faith on the Bible's present knowledge and promise. "Having abolished in his flesh the enmity, even the law of commandments contained in ordinances,"[981] it is that justification by the religious bill is become religious heresy, especially when it is written, "Ye are clean through the word which I have spoken,"[982] and, "If a man love me, he will keep my words."[983]

20. Words, according to the Bible, sanctify. Sanctification by words occur when "rightly dividing the word of truth,"[984] "comparing spiritual things with spiritual."[985] What the illustration of the crucifixion preaches is the limitless boundary of the Bible's words, and the course of that infinite understanding drawing the learner and doer of that knowledge nearer to *creation's* discipline. It is this mentally taxing and soul-anguishing manner of learning that opens up the person to receive the living God's righteousness, which righteousness is to "purge your conscience from dead works to serve the living God."[986]

21. These "dead works" are the spiritual labors of the "dead," and if "the sting of death is sin; and the strength of sin is the law";[987] "dead works" are acts based upon the religious law and tradition of priests and elders. While it is the Bible's intention to redeem the conversation from this error, it is the intention of the spirit and philosophy of the religious world to bring the conversation in to a deeper affiliation with it. The living God's man preaches a resurrection from the dead; refreshing the conversation's mind from the pen of theologians is what is referenced. Wherein, then, are we justified to ignore the fact that this

---

979   Isaiah 53:11
980   Galatians 5:4
981   Ephesians 2:15
982   John 15:3
983   John 14:23
984   2 Timothy 2:15
985   1 Corinthians 2:13
986   Hebrews 9:14
987   1 Corinthians 15:56

"Christ hath redeemed us from the curse of the law, being made a curse for us: for it is written, Cursed is every one that hangeth on a tree"?[988]

22. There is no other intention behind the mediation of this man's philosophy other than the recovery of spiritual understanding from "death's" religious philosophy. Such newness of thought and feeling is important because *heaven's* doctrine has an ultimate aim, seeing as how "the end of the commandment is charity out of a pure heart, and of a good conscience, and of faith unfeigned."[989] The overall wellbeing of the human condition is the living God's will, but since humanity is plagued by "the imagination of the thoughts of the heart,"[990] it is within the conscience of the conversation that this benevolence commences. This is why "that which is born of the Spirit is spirit."[991]

23. The spirit of the mind must regain its consciousness if the person should ever understand its illness, but in order for the mind to live, the mind needs *medicine*, which is why "we have received a commandment from the Father."[992] This commandment is the will and law of creation for a more benevolent personal and devotional government. With our mind finally sober, our heart, and the direction that it should go, will become clear, helping to heal the members of our person because we soberly apply self to what fulfills our character.

24. As human beings, we know fulfillment only when we are able to help cheer and support each other. *Heaven's* commandment is blessed to educate our person to properly care for each other, but not before first learning how to care for self. We can only help any one if we are in a healthy condition to do so, and right aid or charity doesn't begin by what we outwardly do or give, but by where our inward stimulus to help or give originates.

25. I can do and give all day and every day, but I may be doing and giving just for show, which is a symptom of my fellowship with "death": I act for no other reason that to claim *righteousness* by a law of charity.

---

988   Galatians 3:13
989   1 Timothy 1:5
990   1 Chronicles 29:18
991   John 3:6
992   2 John 1:4

Such *righteousness* is not that righteousness of the Bible's present science, which counsels, "Let no corrupt communication proceed out of your mouth, but that which is good to the use of edifying."[993]

26. Edification is the living God's manner of charity, meaning that the living God delights in wisdom and in knowledge, and in discerning wisdom and knowledge, seeing as how "the Spirit searcheth all things, yea, the deep things of God."[994] This "searching" procures mental and spiritual alleviation to our understanding, which is *heaven's* intention. By thoughtfully examining the Bible, an outpouring of blessing will shower our faith's mind, even as it says, "My doctrine shall drop as the rain."[995]

27. When once knowledge of the Bible's doctrine conquers our heart, sobriety will claim our conversation for resurrecting from "death's" practice, which is why we are counseled, "Be ye transformed by the renewing of your mind, that ye may prove what is that good, and acceptable, and perfect, will of God."[996] Our conversation cannot expect to advance if failing to personally examine the Bible's confidence, to do it. "Having abolished in his flesh the enmity, even the law of commandments contained in ordinances,"[997] we today may confidently know that the religious law is religious error[998] to understand what side of the controversy our conversation stands.

28. A great abolishing of the religious law from the living God's philosophy occurred to help the person transcend the religious world to obtain a kind consciousness within self. If we would therefore have the living God's promise of creation, it is well that we learn this promise's science to soberly love the *name* of its Creator, and to edify one another.

---

993 Ephesians 4:29
994 1 Corinthians 2:10
995 Deuteronomy 32:2
996 Romans 12:2
997 Ephesians 2:15
998 1 Corinthians 15:56

29

For Right Service

1. The greatest privilege is found in the saying, "He that overcometh shall inherit all things; and I will be his God, and he shall be my son."[999] Faith's higher education is fully referenced in this quoted verse. The Bible's course of learning is for transcending a very low and popular rendition of that course to capture the remedy given by salvation's science.

2. The science of salvation, to the end the conversation may become useful to other minds sincerely inquiring of the living God's benevolence, is the regeneration and the reformation of the conversation's character. This is why it says, "If any man be in Christ, he is a new creature: old things are passed away; behold, all things are become new."[1000]

---

999   Revelation 21:7
1000   2 Corinthians 5:17

3. The "old" that is passed away is the former manner of devotion through deeds and acts. It is our faith's task to overcome all of these old religious doctrines and habits to possess a fresh learning experience in the living God's present will, which will is to "purge your conscience from dead works to serve the living God."[1001] As our conversation's conscience embraces "Christ" in to it, a sure recovery from the spirit and philosophy of the religious world will take place, opening up the person to the privilege of their faithfulness.

4. The conversation strict to *creation's* present course of learning will inherit every principle of its faith, finding their conversation blessed to fulfill its commission. Every course of learning has a field to occupy, and the conversation joined to the *heavenly Sanctuary's* fellowship is receiving training to become stewards of that Sanctuary's confidence.

5. It is important to allow former religious conceptions and thoughts to pass away because this *Sanctuary* does not honor the religious code of the *world*, as it says, "A greater and more perfect tabernacle, not made with hands."[1002] This *Sanctuary's* assembly passes through a "circumcision made without hands, in putting off the body of the sins of the flesh."[1003] Being without hands, this baptism is evidently not for the physical body, making this *body* of error no physical body. This "body" is the "flesh" or the conversation of our faith, and the Bible's intention is our putting off the error of this *body* to possess a right conversation.

6. "Having abolished in his flesh the enmity, even the law of commandments contained in ordinances,"[1004] this minister has defined "sin," that "the strength of sin is the law."[1005] The religious laws of theologians are the definition of "sin" because they halt faith's sure course of learning, reminding us that "whatsoever is not of faith is sin,"[1006] "and the law is not of faith."[1007]

1001 Hebrews 9:14
1002 Hebrews 9:11
1003 Colossians 2:11
1004 Ephesians 2:15
1005 1 Corinthians 15:56
1006 Romans 14:23
1007 Galatians 3:12

7. The present *circumcision* is in putting off whatever "sin" we possess for owning "salvation through sanctification of the Spirit and belief of the truth."[1008] Because the Bible's sanctification is through mentally and philosophically examining and doing its wisdom; as it says, "Ye are clean through the word which I have spoken";[1009] it is quite necessary to gradually quit subscribing to flesh-based tenets. The persuasion of the religious world is a baptism by hands, or of *righteousness* by way of degrees, commandments, and theories, but with the intended resurrection occurring without hands, it is that our conversation's inwards are "to be strengthened with might by his Spirit in the inner man,"[1010] and "wisdom strengtheneth."[1011]

8. Understanding that right conversion occurs within the conversation's mind, the living God's chief apostle teaches, "That which is born of the Spirit is spirit."[1012] Right sanctification, which is right justification, occurs within the mind, which is why we are counseled, "Be ye transformed by the renewing of your mind, that ye may prove what is that good, and acceptable, and perfect, will of God."[1013]

9. The very essence of this training is contrary to that "old" or former manner of devotion, which counsels one that their wisdom and righteousness comes from the religious law.[1014] The spirit of that "old" service is *righteousness* through the pen of priest and elder: simply do what is written for *blessing* and *favor*, and what is done will be accounted for *faithfulness* to receive *God's* blessing. This train of thought, because *wholeness* appears through doing what is handwritten, is different from that doctrine Abraham exercised, who experienced regeneration not "through the law, but through the righteousness of faith."[1015]

10. While Moses' inspiration moves the person to care to be favorably seen, and to be accounted *righteous* through deed and act,

---

1008 2 Thessalonians 2:13
1009 John 15:3
1010 Ephesians 3:16
1011 Ecclesiastes 3:19
1012 John 3:6
1013 Romans 12:2
1014 Deuteronomy 4:5,6
1015 Romans 4:13

Abraham's philosophy pertains only to a conversation that would be "perfect" or "just," and "perfect, as pertaining to the conscience."[1016] There is no religious law or spiritual tradition in this doctrine or confidence of Abraham, but rather a living experience for cultivating a sober devotional conversation, even as it says, "Be ye holy in all manner of conversation."[1017]

11. A *circumcision* without hands is infinitely more painful than that process with hands, for what wounds on the heart are not dreadful? To walk without knowledge of where to go is painful for most because, if I have no knowledge of what to do, how can I do what to do? But to Abraham, and to the Bible, this logic is faulty, seeing as how it says, "I will bring the blind by a way that they knew not; I will lead them in paths that they have not known: I will make darkness light before them, and crooked things straight."[1018] The Bible, in this statement, shares with us its reasoning behind leading a conversation without any hand-written guide. By not knowing where to go, wisdom will surface for where we should be, keeping our conversation safe.

12. The Bible possesses a philosophy of creation, and this manner of learning; of learning through exercising faith on the Bible's present promise; is its own discipline. Such training allows the mind to create maps of knowledge to guide the heart into the direction it should go. Hereafter we obtain the fashion of the intended conversation, which conversation is of Abraham's *nature*, seeing as how our example "took on him the seed of Abraham."[1019] By wearing the *nature* of Abraham and not of Moses, this man condemns the conversation within the religious world, and so much so that it says, "Christ hath redeemed us from the curse of the law."[1020]

13. We understand the living God's rebuke of Moses' devotional character because this minister's doctrine is given "to redeem them that

---

1016 Hebrews 9:9
1017 1 Peter 1:15
1018 Isaiah 42:16
1019 Hebrews 2:16
1020 Galatians 3:13

were under the law."[1021] And this should be no surprise, for if the pen of priests and ministers were anciently supported then, from Genesis to Exodus, there would be no issue, but since Abraham's *name* was first blessed, since there was no sure and lasting blessing for the hand-written philosophy of Moses, and since his minister, "having abolished in his flesh the enmity, even the law of commandments contained in ordinances,"[1022] teaches us that "the strength of sin is the law,"[1023] the philosophy of the religious law is blatantly condemned. Herein we are made to understand just what our conversation's conscience is to resurrect from, even from "the handwriting of ordinances."[1024]

14. It is for this cause that our *baptism* is without hands, for appetites and passions do not begin outwardly, but rather inwardly. By bringing the Bible's present *voice* into the spirit of our conversation's mind, a renewal of spiritual understanding may commence to help purge our thoughts and feelings from *earth's* confidence to the *heavenly Sanctuary's* higher learning. Henceforward our journey to devotional recovery begins, and if we are faithful, we will receive knowledge of creation's confidence to boldly pronounce it to conversations yet bound in spiritual imprisonment.

15. There is no greater joy than soberly opening up the living God's intention to another inquiring mind. Our hardship against self and against self's character will show forth its goodness when we hear another say, "His spirit was refreshed by you."[1025] The reason why we are now able to bless after the correct manner of blessing is because our conversation has embraced the Bible's educational standard, which standard its chief advocate not only adhered to; saying, "I know him, and keep his saying";[1026] but whose passing and figurative regenerating also bound that standard to this discipline by an exercised faith.

1021 Galatians 4:5
1022 Ephesians 2:15
1023 1 Corinthians 15:56
1024 Colossians 2:14
1025 2 Corinthians 7:13
1026 John 8:55

16. Today, because he dawned the *nature* of Abraham and not of theologians, his offering, while condemning the routine of ministers, magnifies sanctification through an experimental faith on his *saying* as the conversation's mediator. By partaking of this man's devotional joys and sufferings, we are welcomed into his conversation, to learn of its blessing for living that blessing. He, because the philosophy of Moses "was added because of transgressions, till the seed should come to whom the promise was made,"[1027] preached repentance from former religious manners to embrace "the time of reformation."[1028] When once *time* should cast down that flesh-based service and uplift the mind's transformation, the existence of the religious law should pass away; it is become irrelevant due to the fact that our conversation is to be "written not with ink, but with the Spirit of the living God."[1029]

17. Being without ink, the Bible's confidence is without hands, making its circumcision within the spirit of the mind: at this time, "circumcision is that of the heart, in the spirit, and not in the letter; whose praise is not of men, but of God."[1030] Herein is how we inherit all *things* of the Word, or through the living God's *Wisdom*, for by taking on the intended manner of circumcision, all that remains to be acquired are "the commandments of God, and the faith of Jesus."[1031]

18. All *things* concerning the present devotional creation belong to that conversation brought up under the wings of the Bible's present wisdom, and with such training, that conversation may receive the privilege of becoming a minister of the living God's *name*, even as it says, "Behold, what manner of love the Father hath bestowed upon us, that we should be called the sons of God: therefore the world knoweth us not, because it knew him not."[1032] The priests and pastors of the religious world are not the sons or the stewards of this *name* because they have no knowledge of this manner of *love*. This is why it says of them,

---

1027   Galatians 3:19
1028   Hebrews 9:10
1029   2 Corinthians 3:3
1030   Romans 2:29
1031   Revelation 14:12
1032   1 John 3:1

"He hath set the world in their heart, so that no man can find out the work that God maketh from the beginning to the end."[1033]

19. Only conversations that are loved or edified by the Bible's mind can love as that mind edifies, which is why "the Spirit itself beareth witness with our spirit, that we are the children of God."[1034] This type of love is not the love of the religious world. "That good for the sons of men, which they should do under the heaven all the days of their life,"[1035] is spiritual vanity. But to conversations created by the Bible's present discipline, it is that they are "filled with the knowledge of his will in all wisdom and spiritual understanding."[1036]

20. Being filled with the knowledge of the living God's science, it is that this assembly is "full of goodness, filled with all knowledge, able also to admonish one another."[1037] The Bible's "love" is the outpouring of an edifying *rain* upon the understanding, which is why its students are counseled, "Let every one of us please his neighbour for his good to edification."[1038]

21. Being edified, it is that this assembly cares to edify, and this is what separates them as Bible creations. Having inherited the principles of justification, and continuing to exercise their self in those principles, the Bible's creation is created to alleviate hearts and minds. An evident separation from the former, and presently abolished philosophy of the religious world is necessary to claim this benevolence, and for our diligent examination of the Bible's *voice*, it is that we have the opportunity to receive the greatest employment on earth, even bringing redemption's present knowledge to inquiring minds. Because of our willingness to risk our *life*, and to commit that *life* to our faith's *high priest*, we are called to pick up a most noble vocation for human beings.

22. Truth and fact sets the lower human nature on fire, and if we are not faithful to salvation's higher learning, to first observe illness within

---

1033 Ecclesiastes 3:11
1034 Romans 8:16
1035 Ecclesiastes 2:3
1036 Colossians 1:9
1037 Romans 15:14
1038 Romans 15:2

our own self, when confronted with minds more afflicted than our own, we will crumble, or worse, we will compromise salvation's principles to avoid conflict. *Creation's* course is important because by learning how to care for self, we discern how fraudulent the nature of the human being is, allowing us to be able to exercise patience and temperance in thought and in feeling when serving other minds.

23. Charity begins by taking the time to learn how to care for self not according to how self would imagine, but according to redemption's present commandment. Abraham was given only one commandment because he was to know joy as he took personal knowledge of the *voice* within the scriptures, weighing that *voice* with his environment to know just what it said. Today, the same charge given to Abraham is given to our conversation. The living God's chief apostle magnified the *name* of Abraham for the intended promise, and that "name" is understood as being an education "through the righteousness of faith."[1039]

24. The Bible's student gives the wisdom of righteousness by faith through the *name* of this minister, encouraging every conversation to know Bible edification for experiencing *heaven's* benevolent righteousness; this is how we know that we are in the presence of one that is "loved." If we therefore have a seat in the Bible's classroom, it is well to know that our conversation's character is being trained to perform a most charitable task.

25. It is our conversation's task, for possessing a mind that is blessed for right use, to overcome all *things* contrary to the living God's confidence. Every conversation is useful, but it takes time and patience with self to know in just what it is or can be useful. We do not naturally know the Bible's present will or confidence, but we can know it, and we will, if remaining faithful to how it says, "If any man will do his will, he shall know of the doctrine."[1040]

26. Because it is our conversation's assignment to know *creation's* new covenant doctrine, it is well to "be dead with Christ from the rudiments of the world."[1041] We suffer "death" with "Christ" by

---

1039 Romans 4:13
1040 John 7:17
1041 Colossians 2:20

understanding that "Christ," as the *name* is here mentioned, is no reference to a man.

27. It is well to know that "the Lord Jesus Christ our Saviour"[1042] is, in right context, "the commandment of God our Saviour,"[1043] and that by allowing this commandment to devour our conversation's conscience, our transition from the religious world and into the Bible's *Sanctuary* will be made sure. Our experiencing *heaven's* kindness, seeing as how we have a very great commandment to execute, depends upon our conversation immersing its self with this commandment.

1042 Titus 1:4
1043 Titus 1:3